How to b  e

Guidelines for Impr ...
business or start a ....

Franc Ferk

Actor, Producer, Director, Writer and Entrepreneur born in
Europe was trying out new challenges all his life. He
learned it hard way through failures and success.

Edited by **Janet Hayes**
Designed by Franc Ferk & Sergey Pozhilov

Copyright © **Franc Ferk, 2003**
All rights reserved by Franc Ferk through 19, Inc.
ISBN 1-4196-6582-0

This book is dedicated to my loving Parents

Maria & Franc Ferk

Also by Franc Ferk

How to become a millionaire
Future Internet Gurus
Millionaires in Advertising
Car Dealership Millionaires

Accused and Wanted
Aunt Lorraine
Code Developer
Crook
Evil
Fangs
Forever Mine
Freak
Head Hunters
Human Chameleon
Jack S
Jinks
Loser
Maniac
My Daughter
Past Sins
Pistolero
Rahna
Sammo
Satan's Tango
Secret Guardian
Spirit
Teacher
Time Lord
Wiz

If you can't make it with this book, then no one can help you.

The price of the book is set at so low because you are not rich yet. If you are a hardworking individual you'll soon see the results of your work. I won't brag about value – you know the saying "The moon belongs to everyone; the best things in life are free." Paying such a low price is almost free, covering the costs. Good information is always very valuable and if you'll use it the right way you will be on your way up in no time.

This book was written because I always wanted to write a book about what I know and the only thing I can write of is what I did and know best. Others will tell you how they want to help people and share their wealth, oh please give me a break. They want Money, when you get their books you can practically get sick of the simplicity and uselessness of what they wrote. I will not say that I am a good Samaritan who is willing to help everybody. I can only say that helping a few people who really want to change their lives is helping me too (not from selling the book). So if we all can benefit from that why wouldn't I share the Information? All that I ask of you is that while you read this book, please don't skip the chapters, even if it is boring, read it through. People make the biggest mistakes on small things.

In this book you get information on employment opportunities which bring $10,000.00 or more per month. They are not some bogus made up jobs you can't earn a dime with as you usually see with advertisements in Magazines. The book provides list of Companies that offer these opportunities. There are more then 60,000 job openings of this kind so you don't need to worry that they will be taken. You can be a partner, independent

contractor or coworker in business relationships listed in
this book.

Contents

What is missing in your life?

To get Rich, you think probably Money. The question is if you can handle everything that is missing in your life and focus at least a certain amount of time on your success you can be a Manager, maid, bellhop, homemade mom, or anything else, if you follow this book step by step, you can do it. It doesn't matter what education you have, how high your IQ, as long as is over 78 and you can read you'll be fine. This book provides all the "how to" information you need from successfully building a real business on the Net and how to get Organized to Work at Home offers tips on managing your household and family successfully while you work.

Being lazy

If you are lazy, then nothing will work. I have two employees, they were PHP Programmers. The first one was backstabbing, mean and lazy but very intelligent. It didn't work out because his expectations were insane. The second one, who said to me, "I wouldn't have anything, if it wasn't for them helping me out", was just lazy. First of all I paid them for their work and I paid them well. Remember there is always a replacement around the corner you just need to have guts to make a change. I didn't make a change right away and it cost me a lot of Money and Nerves. The second Programmer wasn't that intelligent but he was honest as a person. He wasn't so honest about playing me around saying he is busy and making two weeks of real effective work in five long months. If someone does the work in five months which could and should have been done in two weeks and get paid $5,000.00 per month, what can we call that? Reckless stupidity or intentional fraud? However when I confronted him, he didn't see it this way. He told me before I can pay him later when there will be enough Money, he trusted me. As a person he was great but his logic was: "I don't get paid now so I don't need to work so much or I don't need to work at all, but he still owes me full pay for that time I was on the payroll."

For him it was great logic. So which one do you think was better for the job, the mean, backstabbing one or lazy one with insane logic?

None of them, when you look for staff, look for staff and not for friends. Keep the professional distance with your staff and you'll be fine.

Do you really want to be a millionaire?

Ask yourself! Do you really want to be a millionaire? Are you ready to sacrifice half a year or one year of your life and put in the business what it takes? Are you ready to maintain your wealth on certain level and increasing revenue which is even harder than become a millionaire? If your answer is yes, than go on read the book and after 6 – 12 month write a short review how you did it.

Dying day by day, wasting your life away with a 9 – 5 job

Consider the average American worker. The alarm rings at 7:00 and this worker is up and running. Shower, dress in a professional uniform, sometimes even finds time for breakfast. Usually eating and drinking on the go. Stuck in rush hour traffic going to work and stuck in rush hour traffic going back home from work. Dealing with the boss, coworkers, suppliers, customers wasting his or her life away. Paying bills and being short all the time; struggling week by week, day by day. If you think if my parents managed it and now they are happily retired, so can I, you might be wrong.
Even if you happily retired, why would you waste away the best years of your life, just to be retired at an old age, not so good years of your life? What if your body won't be able to take it? What if you get health problems because of stress, pressure and unhealthy living?

Be a Millionaire now and not in 10 years!

Everybody says you need a lot of time and work to put in. The books you were reading are mentioning decades, investment plans, cutting out expenses, living a simpler life; all that to retire as a millionaire with 1 or 2 million dollars. Not bad? Give me a break, wasting your whole life to be an old millionaire?

It doesn't matter if you are a teenager of legal age or retiree, if you want money you can get it. You have to make up your mind if you are ready to sacrifice half a year to one year of your life to accomplish your goal. Don't put your life totally on hold; you'll break after a few weeks. Don't do drastic changes in your life.

Analyze if you are emotionally fragile, after a divorce, bad break up, bankruptcy, overweight, lost member of the family or dear friend. If you are in 9 – 5 rat race, your present job occupy you too much; don't miss any of details. Put all that on paper.

When you have all your problems on paper try to find a solution for each single problem as a third person who is not affected by the problem. If you can't do it, ask your friends for one or mostly two of your problems and what they think you could do? You'll get a lot of useless answers but some of them might help you to find a solution yourself. Don't tell anyone about your plan, when you start getting more money, don't show it. Don't let anyone interfere with your life, no one can advice you better than you can advice yourself (I'm not talking about professional advices).

Don't ask people how to do things to get on your way to be a millionaire, if they knew they wouldn't be in a 9 – 5 rat race themselves. Remember, no one is more qualified to advise you about your life than yourself. Don't change your life style, don't show you have more money, you'll have a lot of hyenas around you who would want to help you spend your money. Don't give your money to anyone, or lend it to anyone. Others will crush your dreams without even saying thank you. The most you'll get is bad comments when you lose your money. Just keep it to yourself.

Just say no to the rat race! Plan your life! First sit down and think very hard over what you want from your life. When you are clear about what you want from your life than start making a plan.

You did a list of problems, you got more or less OK solutions, now you have to create a plan and stick by the plan. If you can do that you are on your way up.

Here is the Million Dollar Plan

In your list of problems and solutions you must set aside 2 hours per day for your millionaire goal. 1 hour for relaxing, pump yourself up and one hour for work. Pump yourself up; think about things you can do when you reach your goal. Find inner peace, and the will to approach your goal. Remove the thoughts from your head that your friends and family members are telling you.

Almost every innovation is already invented, so inventing something new will be tough. Stick with proven businesses. Where there is enough money for 10 companies from the same industry, there is also enough for eleventh company.

What are you good at? Find your personal niche. Are you into cars, are you good as a Manager, or are you good at Finances, Advertising, Marketing, Promotion, Public Relations, Sales, Entertainment, Human Resources or something else?

Once you decide which way you want to go, then you learn what you can about that industry and do a lot of research. It sounds easy, but it's NOT easy!

First figure it out who are you – if you have Millionaire personality

Don't stick with thoughts about what you think now of who you are. Honestly analyze yourself. If you are not honest with yourself you'll hurt yourself more than you'll help yourself.

Analyze your:

1. Social skills
2. Orientation towards critics
3. Integrity and moral values
4. Creative Intelligence
5. Whether or not you'd rather invest in the stock market or in own business
6. Discipline
7. Intellectual orientation

Can you say to yourself you are with high level of dominance; very competitive and goal oriented, who can be aggressive in resolving uncertainties? Do you have enough sociability which is usually defined by styles of communication? Can you relax? If you can't you'll be having outbursts at the most inappropriate moments. How is your compliance? Can you follow procedures and policies?

Set the goals and build yourself up. You have to put change on paper and start following the plan. Remember old habits die hard, don't get depressed if you don't follow exactly your plan from the first day on. If you are a tough character give yourself a week or two for building up your new business routine, it you are weaker then set your goal to a month to build up your routine.

Stick with the plan and don't make excuses for yourself. If you'll lie to yourself, your plan will fail and you'll feel even more like a loser. At every hard moment compare if it is worth making sacrifices you make now for a short period of time with life time struggles you'll be doing till you retire or drop dead.

Believe me it's easier to suffer one year of than to torture yourself for more than 40 years of struggle and abuse working for someone else.

Define what kind of work would you like to do and figure it out if you are good at that work. You can't be a climber if you weight 300 lbs. You can overcome problems which hold you back from desired kind of work if you can eliminate them in time. You can't do the work which requires abilities you don't posses. You can't be a gymnast if you are 30 years or older, they start at early age. Be realistic with your goals, hey all you have to be is a millionaire and you can start being a millionaire at any and every age.

Don't think about others and how lucky they are having been born with a silver spoon in their mouths. You have to think of you. Thinking of others won't help. What they have and you do not won't help either. You didn't have rich parents, you didn't win a lottery, and you didn't finish College because of lack of money and many more reasons why you are miserable. So what? Who says life is fair? You want something you have to take it.

What ever you start remember knowledge, research, information and persistence are the first steps for you to go. It's not enough just to want something. Let's say you want your own Advertising Agency. What now? You can't just place a sign on your door which says Advertising Agency. You'll fail before you start.

Read some literature about advertising so that you get the idea. When you think you are ready, you are NOT ready yet. Do the research, gather more information, look for failures and look for success stories. Once you are sure of yourself start planning your approach and opening the business.

Don't believe TV commercials how you can easily buy Real Estate with no money down and how you can make millions on Ebay or Google. If it was so easy all Real Estate Agents would be millionaires, all webmasters would be millionaires and all sellers would be millionaires. So who would be poor? Who would work for rich people? It doesn't work this way.

If you are a working mother with kids and without a spouse it may be tough. Not just because of your busy schedule but because of funds being balanced between your business and kids. You can sacrifice your cravings and yearnings for better food, clothes, etc. but you can't say no to kids. Kids need stuff and you can't and shouldn't avoid that. Once you come to a certain financial level the business will go for itself. But yes, you can do it too.

Every business needs some kind of investment. Finances and time for sure. Investment in education, before you start certain business, investment in research, etc.

You can find basics how to start particular business, but being successful will require a lot of work, research and learning.

Start from zero and go for Million or more now

If you have internet access and nothing else, start from zero. First open free email account at Yahoo (if you don't have one already). I'd recommend easy way DeQuba.com. Sign as free Member and test the system. You don't need more than an hour to test the system. Upgrade immediately so you can get through the time limited for fraud protection as soon as possible. Work on the system while waiting for time limited being lifted.

Sell Traffic ($150,000.00/month)

It's very important to refer as many members to your down line as you can. Educate them, teach them what to do, encourage them, work with them. They'll work only if you push them. Remember, it's your business and if you don't take it serious, no one will.

Teach them how to use Ougo Browser and each of them can deliver at least 1000 credits daily, which means 50 credits for you each day from each referral down to 10th level. Focus on 10 or more serious referrals who you will guide, teach them how to form their own groups and guide them. With only 10 serious referrals you'll be able to get in two months more than 5,000.00 credits daily for yourself. You alone will be able to produce more than 20.00 credits daily.

What you can do with 150,000.00 credits monthly?

You can sell them to other Members, which is not the best idea because it's a lot of hassle. Everybody would want to have credits, they promise everything and at the end they negotiate to buy credits for 90%, 80% or even just 70% of the price. Once you locked in your credits, buyer will start negotiating, the buyer knows you are locked in for 30 days and that's how much time the buyer has to get the best deal out of you. You can try out different buyers with smaller amounts of 100 or 200 credits, once you are sure they are OK than you can start to deliver real deal.

Why don't you sell it yourself to an end user? Your 100.00 credits could be sold for $300.00, $500.00 or even $1,000.00 to end buyer. Remember each of your credits is worth 100 hits to the page. 1 hit was evaluated at $0.01 a long time ago, now 1 hit is at least $0.03, usually over $0.10. You have the possibility to create your profile in DeQuba that you can advertise and sell traffic to end users. Most of you will say, they can do it on their own. Tell me one good reason why a company would be doing that, they have their own business and it's easier for them to pay $0.03
per click/hit. You have a lot of referrals who will be happy with their new venture bringing them money. You can even resell your referrals traffic if you run out of your own.

$15,000.00+/month with online car sale

You can create a profile to promote car sales on www.DeQuba.com. The site has specific section where even average people can sell cars. Usually you need a license for every state you want to sell cars, here DeQuba does it for you and you get the commission. It's the easiest way to do it and you don't even need the license. Sign up for Basic Account which is free and than apply for car sales. You'll get all instructions on how and where to start. They'll guide you and help you to earn the most, remember the bigger profits you make the bigger profits they make. The web site for your car dealership would be highly recommended. With the right advertising you might get most of your buyers from the Internet.

$10,000.00+/month as a Payment Processor

Where ever you are located you can become a Payment Processor. The best and easiest money is with finances. Check for all possible payment tools in area where you live. The more payment tools you have, the more customers you'll get. As a Payment Processor you'll be earning and as a Referee from your referrals. As a Payment Processor you'll be charging a fee for every transaction and you'll be getting a fee from DeQuba for every paid membership through your Processing tools. Of course you'll be referring all potential customers through your referral link and you'll be paid also from transfers from your referrals down to 10th level from DeQuba. DeQuba is working on similar system as E-gold only instead of transferring money in gold, platinum and other metals, DeQuba transfers money into Buying Credits (BC). BC can be exchanged for money and has always value 1 BC = $1.00. Selling Credits (SC) are credits which you use for traffic, they can be only sold to other users or used at DeQuba.

DeQuba's Payment Processors are operating as exchange posts, DeQuba doesn't deal with money. The Payment Processor gets the deposit from Members who wants at DeQuba 100 BC (value of $100), the Payment processor charges a small fee for service, which is done locally and Members can reach Payment Processor any time in case of some tricky business. Payment Processor credits its own special account from which Processor transfer desired amount to Members BC account. Members can pay other Members (same as at E-gold), or withdraw them through same or through other Payment Processor as Money in currency he/she wants. It's recommended local Payment Processors so you can visit them and get your Money in cash.

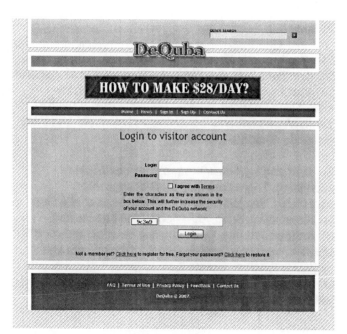

DeQuba

HOW TO MAKE $28/DAY?

Home | News | Sign In | Sign Up | Contact Us

Login to visitor account

Login

Password

☐ I agree with Terms

Enter the characters as they are shown in the
box below. This will further increase the security
of your account and the DeQuba network.

9c3e9

[Login]

Not a member yet? Click here to register for free. Forgot your password? Click here to restore it

FAQ | Terms of Use | Privacy Policy | Feedback | Contact Us

DeQuba © 2007.

www.DeQuba.com

Billions in Advertising

Everybody needs Advertising. Companies, people, charity organizations, and everyone else who want to sale and/or buy Merchandise and/or services. There are many Advertising Agencies out there who are dealing with clients. Agencies with reputation and clientele. What can you do to compete with them?

For start don't get discouraged, they can't cover everything. There are many ways of successful advertising. You just have to find inexpensive, effective and unusual ways fro your clients. You have to find clients too of course. Once you find several neglected but effective ways of advertising, contact the owners and negotiate the deal. Create the packages for your clients. Form a sales Team for your unique advertising which will sell your packages to the clients.

Example:

Property owner owns property close to Interstate Highway, contact the owner, offer him/her a share of advertisements and try to make a deal. Pizza delivery is perfect opportunity to get a spot on their pizza boxes. You split the printing costs with them when you get a client for this kind of advertising. Local Cable Company and local channels are willing and ready to deal with advertisers. Especially if you sponsor an interesting program which will at breaks show your commercial packages. Contact local newspapers which have discounts for Advertising Agencies. Once you create packages for your clients you are ready for business.

One of easiest ways to start with Advertising is of course online. It's one of easiest ways but it's not that easy. Participate first in forums for Pay Per Click Search Engines and read what they talk about. Once you'll figure it out that they in most cases don't know what are they talking about than you are ready for next step.

Find inexpensive code for Pay per Click Search Engine and affordable hosting. Create or ask someone to create a portal with changing keywords which lead to results. Find xml partners who will provide you with xml feed and pay you for that. Forget about Google and Yahoo, even if they by miracle approve you, once you'll start making more than $1,000.00 per day, they'll terminate the contract with you without pay. Yahoo might even pay few percentages from your actual amount but not Google. Use Traffic Brokers like Neterminator.com, Ciazo.com, Svior.com, DeQuba.com and Chounka.com. They are great source of traffic only set them on selected traffic. Once you start making $1,000.00 and more per day, now you are ready for big boys. Read more in next chapters of this book. You can find details in book (Millionaires in Advertising)

Neterminator

Neterminator Home

Program overview

Becoming a Neterminator Partner is simple. With a quick web signup, you will receive a Partner ID as well as auto surf/rotation URL, and referral URL.

It's easy and quite simply the most lucrative way to monetize your traffic you are getting in return. You can get over 100,000 credits per day which you can monetize. If you are using established pay per click programs or you are dealing with private Companies, you can offer them unique clicks per day (no more then 3 clicks/24 hours from same IP or better).

Neterminator.com, an established Online Traffic Broker, delivers targeted Internet traffic to thousands of online web sites every day.

Neterminator.com is not associated with any of web sites which are submitted in Neterminator.com automatic system nor is Neterminator.com responsible for display or content at these web sites. If in rotation appears any web site which is against the law or not in compliance with Terms and Conditions, we ask users who use our free automatic service to report such web sites to authorities.

FAQ • Terms • Privacy • Feedback • Partners

Neterminator @ 2006

www.Neterminator.com

WE ARE LOOKING FOR TRAFFIC BROKERS

RotatorMaster

Corporate   Publishers   Contact Us

LOGIN

Publisher Information

With fastest growing publisher partnerships in the network we are very successful pay per performance network of its kind. Click on Merchant Information or Publisher Information above to find out how you can become part of our winning network today.

PPC Appraisal System offers publishers the ability to sign direct with Merchants.

Ways to use PPC Appraisal System Technology. There are many different sites and business models that find PPC Appraisal System Technology to be a good fit for their needs. Below are some examples of ways we have seen publishers use PPC Appraisal System Technology in the past:

Portfolio sites
These publishers may offer credits back to visitors for purchases made through the sites. These loyalty sites use the Member ID Field to determine which member receives credits or other rewards.

Charity sites
These publishers allow visitors to donate a portion of a purchase to specific organizations. These sites use the Member ID to determine which charity receives which donation.

Member sites
These publishers may provide Web users with different tools and services available to create online environments. These website management sites use the Member ID to track the commerce activity through these sub-sites.

Directories & Search Engines
These publishers may not offer any incentives back to visitors for searching at their site. These loyalty sites use the Member ID to determine which member follow the rules.

Tracking campaigns
Both publishers and merchants have used PPC Appraisal System Technology in order to get more revenue from various campaigns. The Member ID could be used to refer in an email campaign for example.

Sign in now

www.RotatorMaster.com

Publisher.

With fastest growing publisher partnerships in the network we are very successful pay per performance network of its kind. Click on Merchant information or Publisher information above to find out how you can become part of our winning network today.

Please be aware that Partner sites contain some graphic images. You must be an adult, at least 21 years of age and not offended with such images.

Before you sign up YOU MUST read Terms and Conditions!

Becoming a Rigac Partner is simple. With a quick web signup, you will receive a Partner ID as well as URL for sending clicks and referral URL.

Rigac.com, an established Online Traffic Broker, delivers targeted Internet traffic to thousands of online web sites every day.

You must be an adult, at least 21 years of age. You will be exposed to some graphic images. By using and/or viewing this site, you represent and warrant that you have the right, authority, and capacity to enter into this agreement and to abide by all of the terms and conditions of this agreement.

By using and/or viewing this site you represent and warrant under penalty of perjury the following:

That you are an adult, at least 21-years of age

That you will not permit any person(s) under 21-years of age to have access to any of the materials contained within this Site.

That you understand that when you gain access to this site, you will be exposed to visual images, verbal descriptions and audio sounds of a sexually oriented, frankly erotic nature, which may include graphic visual depictions and descriptions of nudity and sexual activity. You are voluntarily choosing to do so, because you want to view, read and/or hear the various materials which are available, for your own personal enjoyment, information and/or education. Your choice is a manifestation of your interest in sexual matters which, you believe, is both healthy and normal and which, in your experience, is generally shared by average adults in your community. You further represent and warrant that you are familiar with the standards in your community regarding the acceptance of such sexually oriented materials, and the materials you expect to encounter are within those standards. In your judgment, the average adult in your community accepts the consumption of such materials by willing adults in circumstances such as this which offer reasonable insulation from the materials for minors and unwilling adults, and will not find such materials to appeal to a prurient interest or to be patently offensive.

That you further represent and warrant that you have not notified any governmental agency, including the U.S. postal service, that you do not wish to receive sexually oriented material.

That you represent and warrant that you have not and will not use and/or view the Site(s) in a restricted location - namely a place, country, or location in which doing so would, or could be deemed a violation of any law, regulation, rule, ordinance, edict or custom.

Except in jurisdictions where such provisions are restricted (and in that event liability is disclaimed to the fullest extent permitted by law), in no event will Company which owns Rigac.com be liable to you or any third person for any indirect, consequential, exemplary, incidental, special or punitive damages, including also lost profits arising from your use of the site or the Rigac service, has been advised of the possibility of such damages. You further agree to hold Rigac.com and Company which owns it including its officers, directors, agents, subsidiaries and employees harmless for claims arising in the event that other user's profile ultimately proves to be offensive, harmful, inaccurate and/or deceptive. Notwithstanding anything to the contrary contained herein, Rigac.com and Company which owns it liability to you for any cause whatsoever, and regardless of the form of the action, will at all times be limited to the amount paid, if any, by you to Rigac.com and Company which owns it for the service during the term of

www.Rigag.com

Program Overview

Becoming a Ciazo Partner is simple. With a quick web signup, you will receive a Partner ID as well as auto surf/rotation URL and referral URL.

It's easy and quite simply the most lucrative way to monetize your traffic you are getting in return. You can get over 100,000 credits per day which you can monetize. If you are using established pay per click programs or you are dealing with private Companies, you can offer them unique clicks per day (no more then 3 clicks/24 hours from same IP or better).

Ciazo.com, an established Online Traffic Broker, delivers targeted Internet traffic to thousands of online web sites every day.

Ciazo.com is not associated with any of web sites which are submitted in Ciazo.com automatic system nor is Ciazo.com responsible for display or content at these web sites. If in rotation appears any web site which is against the law or not in compliance with Terms and Conditions, we ask users who use our free automatic service to report such web sites to authorities.

FAQ • Terms • Privacy • FeedBack • Partners
Ciazo © 2006

www.Ciazo.com

Program Overview

Becoming a Svior Partner is simple. With a quick web signup, you will receive a Partner ID as well an auto surfrotation URL and referral URL.

It's easy and quite simply the most lucrative way to monetize your traffic you are getting in return. You can get over 100,000 credits per day which you can monetize. If you are using established pay per click programs or you are dealing with private Companies, you can offer them unique clicks per day (no more then 2 clicks/24 hours from same IP or better).

Svior.com, an established Online Traffic Broker, delivers targeted Internet traffic to thousands of online web sites every day.

Svior.com is not associated with any of web sites which are submitted in Svior.com automatic system nor is Svior.com responsible for display or content at these web sites. If in rotation appears any web site which is against the law or not in compliance with Terms and Conditions, we ask users who use our free automatic service to report such web sites to authorities.

You must be an adult, at least 21 years of age. You will be exposed to some really disturbing, disgusting pornographic images. By using and/or viewing this site, you represent and warrant that you have the right, authority, and capacity to enter into this agreement and to abide by all of the terms and conditions of this agreement.

By using and/or viewing this site you represent and warrant under penalty of perjury the following:

A) That you are an adult, at least 21-years of age.

B) That you will not permit any person(s) under 21-years of age to have access to any of the materials contained within this Site.

C) That you understand that when you gain access to this site, you will be exposed to visual images, verbal descriptions and audio sounds of a sexually oriented, frankly erotic nature, which may include graphic visual depictions and descriptions of nudity and sexual activity. You are voluntarily choosing to do so, because you want to view, read and/or hear the various materials which are available, for your own personal enjoyment, information and/or education. Your choice is a manifestation of your interest in sexual matters which, you believe, is both healthy and normal and which, in your experience, is generally shared by average adults in your community. You further represent and warrant that you are familiar with the standards in your community regarding the acceptance of such sexually oriented materials, and the materials you expect to encounter are within those standards. In your judgment, the average adult in your community accepts the consumption of such materials by willing adults in circumstances such as this which offer reasonable insulation from the materials for minors and unwilling adults, and will not find such materials to appeal to a prurient interest or to be patently offensive.

www.Svior.com

CHOUNKA

◆ Program overview

Becoming a Chounka Partner is simple. With a quick web signup, you will receive a Partner ID as well as auto surf/rotation URL and referral URL.

It's easy and quite simply the most lucrative way to monetize your traffic you are getting in return. You can get over 100,000 credits per day which you can monetize. If you are using established pay per click programs or you are dealing with private Companies, you can offer them unique clicks per day (no more then 3 clicks/24 hours from same IP or better).

Chounka.com, an established Online Traffic Broker, delivers targeted Internet traffic to thousands of online web sites every day.

Chounka.com is not associated with any of web sites which are submitted in Chounka.com automatic system nor is Chounka.com responsible for display or content at these web sites. If in rotation appears any web site which is against the law or not in compliance with Terms and Conditions, we ask users who use our free automatic service to report such web sites to authorities.

You must be an adult, at least 21 years of age. You will be exposed to some really disturbing, disgusting pornographic images. By using and/or viewing this site, you represent and warrant that you have the right, authority, and capacity to enter into this agreement and to abide by all of the terms and conditions of this agreement.

By using and/or viewing this site you represent and warrant under penalty of perjury the following:

A) That you are an adult, at least 21-years of age

B) That you will not permit any person(s) under 21-years of age to have access to any of the materials contained within this Site.

C) That you understand that when you gain access to this site, you will be exposed to visual images, verbal descriptions and audio sounds of a sexually oriented, frankly erotic nature, which may include graphic visual depictions and descriptions of nudity and sexual activity. You are voluntarily choosing to do so, because you want to view, read and/or hear the various materials which are available, for your own personal enjoyment, information and/or education. Your choice is a manifestation of your interest in sexual matters which, you believe, is both healthy and normal and which, in your experience, is generally shared by average adults in your community. You further represent and warrant that you are familiar with the standards in your community regarding the acceptance of such sexually oriented materials, and the materials you expect to encounter are within those standards. In your judgment, the average adult in your community accepts the consumption of such materials by willing adults in circumstances such as this which offer reasonable insulation from the materials for minors and unwilling adults, and will not find such materials to appeal to a prurient interest or to be patently offensive.

D) That you further represent and warrant that you have not notified any governmental agency, including the U.S. postal service, that you do not wish to receive sexually oriented material.

E) That you represent and warrant that you have not and will not use and/or view the Site(s) in a restricted location - namely a place, country, or location in which doing so would, or could be deemed a violation of any law, regulation, rule, ordinance, edict or custom.

Except in jurisdictions where such provisions are restricted (and in that event liability is disclaimed to the fullest

www.Chounka.com

Millions in Car sales

Cars might be very profitable source of income as long as you know what you are doing. To obtain dealership license will take you from one to two months. You'll need to find space for your car dealership. Office and very small lot will cost you from $500.00 and up per month. Licenses, permits, insurance and bond will cost you about $2,000.00 and than of course phone, office equipment and other expenses another $3,000.00.

How will you sell cars? You have to buy them first. Forget about affordable financing for your newly open car dealership. No one will touch you with a stick. Banks require for other business two years of history for a line of credit, for car dealerships 5 years of history. If you get good friend you can involve them and split profit with them for their investment. One of better ways to do it is to accept cars on consignment. People bring their cars, they still have insurance and they'll pay you from sale 6% - 10%. Once you get enough money for buying and selling cars, you'll be probably hitting to the auctions for car dealers.

Promote your business through newspapers, online, flyers; ask your friends to spread the word, especially if they are financially involved. By consignment sale you'll be using other people money for your benefit while providing them with service. Sale only 20 cars per consignment per month and you'll be making between $12,000.00 and $20,000.00 per month.

Important is to establish contacts with other car dealers. When ever you need a particular car you make some phone calls and probably find it for your customer. Especially if you offer also car brokerage services where you find and sell particular cars for your clients.

Buying at the auctions doesn't always mean biggest commission. Depends on the auction where you are buying. Sometimes pay off to do the research where particular Makes and Models are cheaper and where more expensive. In such case you can buy them at one Auction and sell them at the other Auction. Profits will be smaller but as long as are profits is OK.

You have to inspect the car before buying it. First do that one day before the auction where is possible and than again before auction just in case if something got broken in the mean time.

Export cars is nowadays much easier than it was. You can find dealers from foreign countries online who will buy American cars. As long as you prepare all papers necessary and make a list of to do things everything should go smooth.

For easier start you can look up for people who doesn't have dealer license and want to buy and sale cars. They'll be more than willing to pay you a commission for such a silent umbrella dealership.

Don't forget to make a deal with lenders and financial companies, especially those who finance people with bad credit. There are many more things you have to be careful and easiest way you can find details in book (Car Dealership Millionaires)

www.Autoraw.com

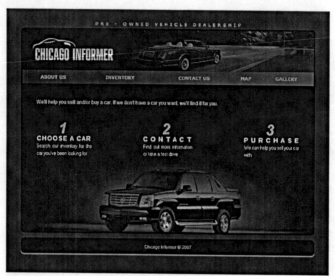

www.ChicagoInformer.com

Easy wealth in Online Business

You have to know the basics before you start making Money. Sales are one possibility. You can resale products, there are many Companies offering Affiliate and Partnership programs. It's true you can make your own product but then you are limited with how much you can produce.
When you start your online business pay attention to few important things. If you decide to create your own web site you have to find first affordable and reliable hosting like www.bulkregister.com, then you need reliable and affordable hosting like www.datapipe.com. One of important things is design and website crated user friendly. Adding a newsletter doesn't hurt and including Meta Tags would be strongly recommended.

Speed up your web site, make it easy for prospective buyers to find what they are looking for, make your web pages easy to read, and make it easy to contact you. Follow these tips to make your web site user friendly and increase sales.

User Friendly

Speed up your web site. Your web sites speed has a significant impact on user loyalty. A slow web site will cost you sales. Visitors wont wait more than 8 seconds for your web pages to load. Make your home page fast loading to keep visitors at your site.

Make it easy for prospective buyers to find what they are looking for. Easy navigation is essential to keeping prospective buyers at your site. Provide plenty of links on your home page, giving visitors an overview of your web sites content and choices. Provide links to your home page and main sections such as order form, contact page, products, and articles on every page. Visitors may not visit your pages in the sequence you would like them to. Provide a site map or table of contents if your site has more than 10 pages. Make sure all links are working.

Make your web pages easy to read. An easy to read, professionally designed web site can maximize your sales. Use color and spacing to make your web pages easy to read. Dark text on a light background is easy to read. A hint of color softens the screen. Avoid text on dark and busy backgrounds. Break up your sales copy into short, easy to read sections and use subheadings to highlight benefits. Split up long pages into several pages.

Keep pages short. Visitors should be able to see the important information, especially on your home page, without scrolling down. Studies show that more than half of the web surfers never scroll down past the first screen of information, so provide your benefits, site description, and USP at the top of the page.

Make it easy to contact you. Provide your phone number, email address, and URL (web address) on every page. This will make it easier for people to go back to your web site.

A user friendly site will sell more. Make your web site user friendly to keep visitors at your site, read your sales materials and buy from you.

Copy that converts visitors into buyers You're getting lots of visitors, but not a lot of sales. How can you increase the number of buyers without increasing traffic? Design, usability and layout have an impact on sales, but your words are what really sell — or don't.

Start by evaluating your web copy. If you were a stranger visiting your website, would you believe your offer? Is it worth the price you are charging for it? If not, it's time to reevaluate your offer.

You must overcome risk — when shopping online, customers can't touch or feel your product like they can in a store. So you have to communicate the VALUE of your offer. Tell them how they will benefit and how much they are getting for their money.

Another way to overcome risk is to offer a guarantee. "100% money-back guarantee. If you're not satisfied for any reason, we will refund your money, no questions asked." Lessening the risk involved in buying your product puts your customers at ease and opens their minds to buying.

Reassure them on other pages of your website and on your order form.

If you're in a service business where customers can't return the product, and then guarantee the solution you provide. For example, a graphic designer could guarantee that the project is completed on time and budget. A plumber may guarantee that your pipes won't leak anymore.

Guaranteeing your work shows that you stand behind your claims and believe in your products.

Another way to entice visitors to buy is by offering free samples. Sweeten the deal with something free and you are sure to gain your prospects' attention. Offer a free trial subscription to your magazine, a free three-day supply of your wrinkle cream, or a free estimate. Service businesses can offer a free consultation or "how-to" booklet.

Give details. Write exciting, interesting descriptions next to each product photo (you do have photos up, right?).

Include as many details as you can. The more information a prospect has, the more she/he will trust you.

Solve problems. Let visitors know what problems your product or service solves. Don't be afraid to describe the problems. Once you do that, show visitors what their life will be like after they buy your product. Tell them how your customers use your product and benefit from it — visitors will identify with real life examples.

Are there testimonials on your web site? Nothing enforces your credibility more than other customers' experiences. Whenever you get complimentary letters or emails from satisfied customers, ask their permission to reprint them. Including their first and last names along with their companies and cities where they live enhances credibility.

Focus your copy. It is said that people don't read on the net. Don't take this to mean that your copy can be sloppy and generic. If in doubt, hire someone else to write it for you. Be specific with details. It is also said "The more you tell, the more you sell." Provide prospects with lots of information on a well-written site.

Finally, capture your visitors' email addresses. In exchange for their email addresses, offer something free, such as an ezine, updates on special offers or free information. (You can automate this by setting up an auto responder.) When you obtain their permission to contact you, you are able to follow up with them later and build a relationship. Over time, they will get to know and trust you and you will have a better chance of making a sale.

When you evaluate your website copy, you may find any number of things that can hinder your sales, but mostly it will be your copy. Make these simple improvements to your words and you offer and you will sell more.

What attract buyers? Attract Potential Buyers to Your Web Site with Content.

Give People a Reason to Visit Your Web Site

Content is the most important part of your Web site. Useful content gets visitors to your site, engages them, and builds credibility. Surveys indicate that sixty-five percent of visitors go to Web sites to get information. Only five percent are interested in graphics.

Valuable content can include how-to articles, reports, tips, and even links to relevant sites providing useful resources. For example, a Web design company may provide free graphics and diagnostic tools. A CD Web site may offer free reviews, biographies of musicians, and an online jukebox that allows visitors to preview their music selection.

To make money with your Web site, you also need to include:

Contact information. Include your name, business name, email, 800#, local phone number (international prospects can't call 800 numbers), fax, and mailing address.

Company information.

Information about your products or services (tips for buying your products or services). A compelling sales letter.

Special offer.

A call to action (click here to see examples of action words).

Order information (tell prospects how to order). An online order form (include links to your order form and sales letter on your home page). Target Your Audience

Provide information that is valuable, useful, or entertaining to your target market.

Feature content relevant to the topic of your site.

Use a feedback form to find out what your visitors want.

Visitors typically come to your Web site four to five times before they buy from you.

Our next report reveals how to attract visitors back to your site.

This article is excerpted from Inside Secrets to Developing a Profitable Web Site.

Click here for more information.

Make easy profit

Step 1: Determine Your Purpose

The first step in planning a web site is to determine what you want to accomplish. Do you want to sell products and services, find new customers, establish credibility, or improve customer service?

The purpose of your web site will affect its content and design. Depending on your goal, you may want to write articles to establish trust, provide a compelling sales letter, a catalog, product information, a secure online order form, and a shopping cart.

Step 2: Define Your Ideal Customers, Their Needs and Concerns

Many web sites are trying to attract everybody. Dont make this mistake. Your web site will be more profitable when focusing on your ideal prospects who are likely to buy your products or services. Ask the following questions to create a profile of your ideal customers.

- Who are your customers? Who will be visiting your web site?

- Who wants or needs your products or services?

- What are your customers needs and concerns?

- What is the age range, gender, profession, industry, income level, education, and reading level of your ideal customers?

- Why will they come to your site?

- What problems do your products or services solve?

- What information do they want?

- Are most of your customers computer literate?

- What computer, monitor, and screen resolution do they have?

- What browsers do they use?

- Do your visitors connect to the Internet with a slow modem or a fast connection such as cable or DSL?

After defining your ideal customers, target your web sites content, message, and design directly to them. Here are some examples of how your audience affects the design of your web site. If you are targeting seniors, make your text large. If your prospects are accountants, use a conservative design. Make your design colorful for children. Avoid movies, sounds, Flash animations, and Java programming if your clients have slow computers and Internet connections.

To target your content to your ideal customers, tell right away what your web site is about and what's in it for them. If they don't read further, they were not prospects. Attract your target audience with a benefit-oriented headline and provide valuable, useful, and interesting information your prospects are interested in.

Step 3: Demonstrate Your Uniqueness

Emphasize your uniqueness to make your web site stand out and set you apart from your competition. Attract your audience with a benefit that is different from other web sites. What is your distinct advantage? What separates you from your competition? What is distinctive about your offer? Why should your prospects choose you over others?

Visiting competing web sites will give you ideas about content, design, and features you may need for your web site. Than develop a site that stands out and distinguishes you from them.

Answer these questions to help you formulate your uniqueness.

- What are the most important results your customers will achieve from your products or services?

- Why should prospects buy from you instead of your competitors?

- What do you do better than anyone else? Do you possess hard-to-find or specialized expertise? Do you offer a free consultation, initial visit, analysis, or better advice?

- What makes your products or services better, unique, or more desirable than your competitors?

- Do you have the lowest prices or the highest quality products in your industry? Do you provide the fastest service, the strongest guarantee, longest hours, or better follow up? Do you keep customers informed with newsletters or information hotlines?

Plan your web site for profits. Determine what you want to accomplish with your web site, who your ideal audience is, and what makes your online business unique. Only after implementing these steps are you ready to start developing your web content.

Good to avoid

Geared Up with a website and lots of energy to make a mark online? Spare some time and go through this. You'll be glad you did. If you don't already, this is something you MUST know!

1. Maintain a Navigational system throughout your website easy to follow.

2. Do not use frames unless it's really important. Visitors detest getting stuck up in frames and Search Engines find it difficult to index websites with frames.

3. Avoid using scrollbars horizontally. There is nothing more annoying than having to scroll both vertically and horizontally at all screen lengths.

4. A full Flash Website may look very appealing, but that's the last thing your visitors are going to wait for to load. Instead try embedding Flash on your pages to get the same look.

5. To minimize download time, use tables with different background colors to add life to your pages, instead of using too many graphics.

6. Do not cluster too many animated buttons and banners throughout your site. Your visitors will not be able to browse comfortably with all that blinking going on and will surf elsewhere.

7. Keep updating your website. People will not return if they find the same old stuff lying there.

8. Put up a message board, feedback form, guestbook etc. to add a touch of interactivity to your website.

9. Make it a point to return the visits and/or answer all e-mails/messages within a reasonable period of time.

10. Provide links to other websites, even your competitors, if possible. This shows you are not conceited and are willing to help your visitors to find what they need. This little gesture goes a long way to earn you goodwill. When you have your website ready you can earn up, to $50.00 per month if you are lucky. Depends how good you are. More recommended is to find Affiliate and Partnership programs which help you to earn money, to earn solid income every month.

Ways to get your wealth as an Internet Guru

Flat Commission Program

Most of affiliate programs have a flat commission on all referred sales, the occasional affiliate marketing program will seem like a twisting weird bunch of conditions and requirements. The truth is that while it isn't impossible to earn a decent living without a complete understanding of how the money is coming in, it's good to understanding the mechanics of your affiliate program will reveal where to direct your effort to realize the most profit for the time you invest in your online business.

Multi level Marketing Affiliate Program

A Multi level Marketing Affiliate Program is one of the easiest programs to understand. When you introduce a new affiliate to the program, they become your direct referral, or sub-affiliate. There is no limit to the number of sub-affiliates you can have and in addition to the commission you earn on your personal sales, some programs will pay you a smaller commission on the sales of your direct referrals, so called a second-level or second-tier commission. If your direct referrals also introduce new affiliates to the program and you earn a commission on their sales, a third-tier commission is being paid. Theoretically, there is no limit to the number of levels a compensation program could pay you on, but in practice most online affiliate programs only pay a commission on one or two tiers. This is largely to separate affiliate programs from the often-maligned multi-level marketing.

Spill over Multi level Marketing Affiliate Program

One of the biggest problems with Multi level Marketing Affiliate Program is that anyone who becomes successful

recruiting direct referrals will quickly have too many to communicate with regularly. Since regular interaction with your up line is a key to success for many affiliates, some program managers choose to implement a Spill over Multi level Marketing Affiliate Program. In a spill over Multi level Marketing Affiliate Program is a set number of direct referrals you may have. If you continue to recruit new affiliates after you have reached that limit, they will "spill over"
to become sub-affiliates of your direct referrals. Since you are restricted in how many direct referrals you may have, spill over Multi level Marketing Affiliate Program generally pay on more tiers than Multi level Marketing Affiliate Programs.

One of the goals of a spill over Multi level Marketing Affiliate Program is to create an environment in which every new affiliate has a mentor immediately above them with the time to offer training and guidance. This is partially successful, but can be disorienting for new affiliates who are recruited in to the program by someone who has earned their trust only to be handed over to another program member who may or may not maintain that same rapport. A spill over Multi level Marketing Affiliate Program also produces freeloaders who wait for spillover affiliates and fail to do any recruiting of their own.

Power line Multi level Marketing Affiliate Program

Whether it's called a Power line Multi level Marketing Affiliate Program, or something entirely different, this program is often made to sound far more complicated than it really is. Imagine a spill over Power line Multi level Marketing Affiliate Program where you are limited to only one direct referral. If you recruit a second sub-affiliate, she spills over beneath the first. A diagram of your down line will resemble a straight line. If there is a limit on how many levels down you earn a commission, you quickly run out of motivation to recruit new affiliates. The solution is usually to pay you a commission on all sales made by anyone in your down line for an infinite number of levels.

Breakaway

If you are participating in a pay line program that pays a 10% commission, some quick calculations will quickly reveal that once the 10th level affiliate is referred to the program and makes a sale, the company is paying out the entire price of the product or service in affiliate commissions. Since that business model will quickly destroy any company, pay line programs that pay on infinite levels must have some sort of breakaway, sometimes called stair step breakaway. When one of your sub-affiliates meets a certain criteria (usually personally recruiting some number of new affiliates) they break away from your line and start their own pay line. When
this happens, you no longer receive a commission on the activity of their direct referrals.

Override Commission

If that were the end of the story, there wouldn't be much incentive to mentor your sub-affiliates and teach them how to recruit people to the program. Therefore, breakaway plans almost always have an override commission. Whenever one of your referrals breaks away, you still receive a small commission on their activity. Usually breaking away also signifies a graduation on the part of your sub-affiliate to a point where they will require less guidance from you.

If none of these concepts sound like a perfect match for a compensation plan you know about, it's because most affiliate program managers customize these elements to create a unique compensation plan. Examining a compensation plan will provide clues about the objectives of the program manager and what direction they plan to take the affiliate program in the future.

Ultimate Power line Multi X Level Marketing Affiliate Program

This program has 10 levels with 5% on each level or 20 levels with 3% on each level. You can refer as many Affiliates you want and they may refer as many affiliates they want, as long as they are in one of 1st - 10th level in your down line they'll be bringing you 5% commission or one of 1st - 20th level in your down line they'll be bringing you 3% commission. Imagine this kind of potential. Many times those two programs are misused from Individuals. Some Individuals sign in 10 or 20 levels all owning all 10 or 20 accounts signed under each other. That's how they accomplish maximum payout of 50% or 60%. They are working with the Account at the last level of their own chain of Accounts. Companies with that kind of programs protect themselves with setup, activation and training fee to prevent misuse. It's symbolic fee of maybe $10 – $30 and most of scammers think twice to signup 10 or 20 times and pay $ 100 – 600.

Affiliate program

You have to find a good one which will pay you for visitors who come back long time after first visit. A cookie is just a little text file that basically labels your computer as having been to particular web site and it can be also seen who referred the Visitor. If person X comes to a web site with person Y's affiliate ID, a little text file is dropped on their computer pointing out that person X visited as result of clicking at persons Y link. If the person X ever comes back cookie is ready and if any sale or other action is made, it's credited to person Y. Not many people clear their cookies from the browser. It's important how you give away your commission, instead of giving away just 30% it's in many cases smarter to give away 2 or 3 tier commission let say 1st level 13%, 2nd level 10% and 3rd level 7%. Affiliates will have incentive to refer other potential Affiliates and 10 people can do much more than one. Affiliates who referred few new Affiliates will start getting commission popping out from no where and they'll be even more motivated to get more and more people. It's difficult to choose the right most beneficiary Affiliate Program. Big companies are making Affiliate Programs less and less beneficial

Promote your business

Popups

Popup works if you use it right. It works better then popunder. Most of the people find popups annoying and disturbing. Popups got bad reputation mostly because they are used from porn sites which are sending army off different popups which you can't close and if you close them they create a new army of popups.

If the popup is used correct it will bring desirable results. Many big Companies are using popups, popunders, slideins, peeloffs, etc. If you can buy cheap popups or popunders it might work for you with a solid profit.

Email Campaigns

Same is with email Campaigns, people hate them even when they subscribe for them they'll in the most cases still hate Campaigns. It's important how and who you choose for Email Campaign. There are many scam artists out there who will take your money and you can't do anything about it Some will actually send your message but through spam and your site can get shut down for that or you'll at least get whole bunch of problems.

If you send advertising through Paid Emails you'll find thousands of them on internet, do it just through few biggest ones, because some Affiliates are in 10 or more different Paid Email data bases. So you'll be sending same message to the same person only paying 10 times more.

If there would be reliable and affordable Advertising Company on internet they would make a fortune. All companies even the biggest are promising visitors, potential buyers, conversions, perfect ROI. You'll be getting hits from Pay per Click Search Engines (PPC SE) you never heard about. They'll charge you every click, even fraudulent ones, they won't pay those PPC SE's for all clicks and they'll be making out like a bandit.

Massive Frauds

Massive Frauds in the Affiliate Programs that are taking place with the casino and other affiliate programs controlled by the crooked organized crime operators. Many of them are located overseas and even if report are based on extensive research, testing, reporting, complaints, investigations, compiled for the certain amount of time and the source of these information comes from Affiliate program developers, their own directors and officers, their management and accountants, their technical support and sales teams, their marketing companies, their licensees, their affiliates, and also their own players, than you can't ignore it anymore. Many affiliate programs don't track the real sales properly, and most don't track them at all. Plenty of massive frauds, and figures confirming that 96% or 100% of the sales are not tracked at all, so the poor innocent affiliates got massively cheated and robbed by these thieves.

There are also plenty of companies who run these dishonest affiliate programs based on cheating, and defrauding the affiliates. Their entire business models are based on frauds, and nothing else than frauds. As upset and disappointed affiliates leave after two or three month company already got 5 times more new affiliates who are sending traffic.

Thousands of naive affiliates wrongly think that bigger is better, so they sign up with the bigger ones. The fact is that the biggest ones are sometimes the worst, and they are only bigger because they cheated and defrauded more affiliates and more players with their fraudulent rigged software. Many "big boys" cheat, even well known names.

Developers play dumb but it is absolutely certain that the developers are heavily involved with these massive frauds, together with their own licensees with their marketing companies. This is pure and straight organized crime at a massive level. The smart webmasters and affiliates are dropping these fraudulent scams and insisting on pay per click and pre paid advertising. The others are getting massively cheated, more than they can ever imagine. If you sign for affiliate program, track the feedback in forums and track your own activities.

Few sources to start immediately

1. Start as an Affiliate and become a Franchisee

Job Queen, Do Careers, Job Monarch or Careers King coworker

Job Queen (www.jobqueen.com) has unique Affiliate program which pushes Affiliate to do the best he/she can. You can become a Job Queen Franchisee by paying for Franchise or getting it as the most successful contractor (Affiliate, Recruiter or Recruiter Manager). Job Queen has 10 tier payment scale 5% for each level in Affiliates down line. Profits you can make, with a little work and a little Internet knowledge, are incredible.

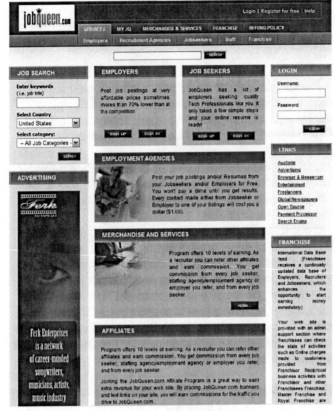

JOB SEARCH

Enter keywords
(i.e. job title)

Select Country
United States

Select category:
– All Job Categories –

SEARCH

ADVERTISING

Ferk

Ferk Enterprises
is a network
of career-minded
songwriters,
musicians, artists,
music industry

EMPLOYERS

Post job postings at very affordable prices sometimes mores than 70% lower than at the competition.

SIGN UP   SIGN IN

JOB SEEKERS

JobQueen has a lot of employers seeking quality Tech Professionals like you. It only takes a few simple steps and your online resume is ready!

SIGN UP   SIGN IN

EMPLOYMENT AGENCIES

Post your job postings and/or Resumes from your Jobseekers and/or Employers for Free. You won't pay a dime until you get results. Every contact made either from Jobseeker or Employer to one of your listings will cost you a dollar ($1.00).

MERCHANDISE AND SERVICES

Program offers 10 levels of earning. As a recruiter you can refer other affiliates and earn commission. You get commission from every job seeker, staffing agency/employment agency or employer you refer, and from every job seeker.

MORE

AFFILIATES

Program offers 10 levels of earning. As a recruiter you can refer other affiliates and earn commission. You get commission from every job seeker, staffing agency/employment agency or employer you refer, and from every job seeker.

Joining the JobQueen.com Affiliate Program is a great way to earn extra revenue for your web site. By placing JobQueen.com banners and text links on your site, you will earn commissions for the traffic you drive to JobQueen.com.

LOGIN

Username:

Password:

LOGIN

LINKS

Auctions
Advertising
Browser & Messenger
Entertainment
Freelancers
Global Newspapers
Open Source
Payment Processor
Search Engine

FRANCHISE

International Data Base feed (Franchisee receives a continually updated data base of Employers, Recruiters and Jobseekers, which enhances the opportunity to start earning money immediately)

Your web site is provided with an admin support section where franchisees can check the stats of activities such as Online charges made to customers provided from Franchisor Reciprocal business activities with Franchisor and other Franchisees Franchise, Master Franchise and Royal Franchise are

www.JobQueen.com

Explanation they have for Recruiter Managers, Recruiters and Affiliates:

Recruiter Manager

A Recruiter Manager works per commission during a 3 month probation period. Work is strictly online and contains, besides forming Recruiter Teams contacting Companies/Employers for Corporate accounts, contacting Schools and Colleges for participation of their students, Recruitment Agencies to upload their database. During the first month the Recruiter Manager should be able to form a team of 20 Recruiters and train them to do the work. The Recruiter
should, within the first month, referred few Companies, Recruitment Agencies and over 10 Affiliates and 30 Jobseekers.   Work contains contacting individuals (potential Jobseekers, Affiliates and Recruiters) Companies, Colleges and Recruitment Agencies. While contacting them Recruiter Managers present them the benefits and why join us. Each Recruiter Manager has to report on daily basis in Forum and list the sources where he/she placed the ads and what was the response.

Recruiter Manager covers particular area and place the ads in that area. Ads are placed for Recruiters. Companies, Recruitment Agencies and Colleges are contacted direct. Recruiter Manager should refer at least few Companies, Recruitment Agencies and Colleges to get the feeling for the job. Recruiter Manager will be unable to explain to Recruiters how and what to do if he/she won't have own experience. Potential Recruiters are usually recruited through online and offline Classifieds, Forums and Groups. Recruiter Managers should train as many Recruiters, during the probation period, that they can. Striving to form a team of 20 to 30 Dynamic, Aggressive and hard working Recruiters.

Online Training involves presenting a working plan to Recruiters, monitor them through their reports and work, help and direct them, suggest whereto advertise, getting feedback from them and than help them out. The Recruiter Manager is obligated to post a short report every working day from Monday to Friday to the General Manager of the Sales and Recruitment Department. During the probation period the Recruiter Manager should be recruiting new recruits all the time and at the end successful Recruiters who meet the deadlines will be chosen. Every Recruiter
Manager's log, comment and posting will be saved in the Forum where the communication will take place.

Recruiter Manager must be familiar with Recruiter and Affiliate work, otherwise he/she is not able to monitor and guide Recruiters and advice them about Affiliates. Every Recruiter Manager is obligated to check in forum on daily basis and report to General Manager. When ever Recruiter Manager signs up a new Recruiter, he/she must sign through Recruiter Managers tracking URL. All tracking is done automatic and online. The same goes for Employers, Recruitment Agencies and Colleges, all those participants should sign either through referral URL or type in the Promo Code of Recruiter Manager. If the Recruiter Manager is earning less than $6,000.00 per Month after 3 Months period, than it's something wrong. You must know that one from 6 Recruiter Managers is successful and stays as permanent Employee.

Recruiter

The Recruiter works the first 3 months of the probation period on commission referring Jobseekers, Recruitment Agencies and Employers. From Recruiter is expected in first month to recruit at least 30 Affiliates, 30 Jobseekers, 10 Companies and 2 Recruitment Agencies.

The Recruiter works on recruiting every working day from Monday to Friday And focuses on getting as many Affiliates as possible. Recruiters must beware that they need to contact while recruiting Affiliates, Companies and Recruitment Agencies. One database of Recruitment Agency brings more Employers, Jobseekers and potential Affiliates than one Recruiter is able to get in 6 month. Work contains contacting individuals (potential Jobseekers, Affiliates and Recruiters) Companies, Colleges and Recruitment Agencies.

While contacting them Recruiter Managers present them the benefits and why join us. Each Recruiter has to report on daily basis in Forum and list the sources where he/she placed the ads and what was the response. Recruiter covers particular area and place the ads in that area. Ads are placed for Affiliates. Companies, Recruitment Agencies and Colleges are contacted direct. Recruiter should refer at least 70 Companies, 6 Recruitment Agencies and 3 Colleges in probation period get the feeling for the job.

Recruiter will be unable to explain to Affiliates how and what to do if he/she won't have own experience. Potential Affiliates are usually recruited through online and offline Classifieds, Forums and Groups. Recruiters should train as many Affiliates, during the probation period that they can. Striving to form a team of 20 to 30 Dynamic, Aggressive and hard working Affiliates. Online Training involves presenting a working plan to Affiliates, monitor them through their reports and work, help and direct them, suggest whereto advertise, getting feedback from them and than help them out. The Recruiter is obligated to post a short report every working day from Monday to Friday to the Recruiter Manager.

During the probation period the Recruiter should be recruiting new Affiliates all the time and at the end successful Affiliates who meet the deadlines will be chosen. Every Recruiter's log, comment and posting will be saved in the Forum where the communication will take place.

Recruiter must be familiar with Affiliate work, otherwise he/she is not able to monitor and guide Affiliates and advice them about work. Every Recruiter is obligated to check in forum on daily basis and report to Recruiter. When ever Recruiter signs up a new Affiliate, he/she must sign through Recruiters tracking URL.

All tracking is done automatic and online. The same goes for Employers, Recruitment Agencies and Colleges, all those participants should sign either through referral URL or type in the Promo Code of Recruiter. Recruiter should be earning at least $3,700.00 per Month after 3 Months period, if not than it's something wrong. One from 10 Recruiters is successful and stays as permanent Employee and 3 from 5 permanent Employees/Recruiters become Recruiter Managers.

Affiliate

There are two kinds of affiliates, active and passive. Passive Affiliates sign up, refer few new Affiliates and stops. Active Affiliate works almost as the Recruiter, referring new Affiliates, Jobseekers, Recruitment Agencies and Employers only on less professional level than Recruiter. Good Affiliates are offered permanent Recruiter positions.   Jobseekers, Recruitment Agencies and Employers sign up for free. Recruitment Agencies and Employers can operate two ways: they can make a free posting and when Jobseekers contact them, they pay per each contact for already reviewed resume, $1.00 or they can make a posting for $20.00 -$30.00 and Jobseekers will contact them directly. In first case they do not pay before they get the results and in second case they pay very affordable price for job posting.

Potential Affiliates should sign up as Jobseekers at www.jobqueen.com/register_user.php, upload their Resumes and Activate their Accounts. Once they are done contact Company for online training.

Active Affiliate start making after a Month or two couple of hundred dollars per month and then it grows to thousand and couple of thousand dollars per Month. 7 from 10 active Affiliates become Recruiters.

If you try Job Queen you have to try these three too. It's the same system with few smaller differences you only quadruple the earnings.

Do Careers (www.docareers.com)

They have also 10 Tier Affiliate Program which has first 5 levels 5% each and second 5 levels 4% each. Rules are similar than by Job Queen. It seems to be a small percent per each level, but when you do the math the numbers are enormous. With a solid start you can start pulling couple of thousand per week in less then a month.

Level	%
1	5
2	5
3	5
4	5
5	5
6	4
7	4
8	4
9	4
10	4

Try to prove yourself as an active affiliate and then apply for Manager position, which brings even more money, because you'll have access to inside information.

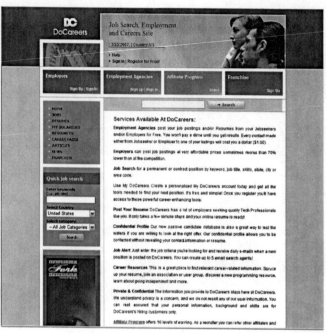

www.DoCareers.com

Job Monarch (www.jobmonarch.com)

They have also 10 Tier Affiliate Program with 10 levels:

Level	%
1	3
2	4
3	6
4	5
5	4
6	3
7	3
8	2
9	2
10	1

Rules are similar than by Job Queen and Do Careers. If you tried those you can use the same team you form before and they'll do just fine for you.

JobMonarch
JOBMONARCH.COM

| Home | Jobs | Resumes | My JobMonarch | Resources | Career Fairs | Articles | News | Franchise |

Job Search
Employment
and Careers

Job Search

Job Search for a permanent or contract position by keyword, job title, skills, state, city or area code.

My JobMonarch

Create a personalized My JobMonarch account today and get all the tools needed to find your next position. It's free and simple! Once you register you'll have access to these powerful career-enhancing tools.

Confidential Profile

Our new passive candidate database is also a great way to test the waters if you are willing to look at the right offer. Our confidential profile allows you to be contacted without revealing your contact information or resume.

Job Alert

Just enter the job criteria you're looking for and receive daily e-mails when a new position is posted on JobMonarch. You can create up to 5 email search agents!

Career Resources

This is a great place to find relevant career-related information. Spruce up your resume, join an association or user group, discover a new programming resource, learn about going independent and more.

Private & Confidential

The information you provide to JobMonarch stays here at JobMonarch. We understand privacy is a concern

Employment Agencies

Post your job postings and/or Resumes from your Jobseekers and/or Employers for Free. You won't pay a dime until you get results. Every contact made either from Jobseeker or Employer to one of your listings will cost you a dollar ($1.00).

Sign Up | Sign In

Employers

Post job postings at very affordable prices sometimes mores than 70% lower than at the competition.

Sign Up | Sign In

Post Your Resume

Would you or any of your friends like a $100? If your resume is randomly picked by our company you win $100, and the person who referred you will get $50

Sign Up

Affiliate Program

Program offers 10 levels of earning. As a recruiter you can refer other affiliates and earn commission. You get commission from every job seeker, staffing agency/employment agency or employer you refer, and from every job seeker, staffing agency/employment agency or employer they refer down through the 10th level.

Enter

Job Search

Quick Search

[   ]

Search

Enter keywords
(i.e. job title)

[   ]

Select Country
United States

Select category
– All Job Categories –

Search

www.JobMonarch.com

Careers King (www.careersking.com)

They have also 10 Tier Affiliate Program with 10 levels:

Level	%
1	5
2	6
3	7
4	5
5	4
6	4
7	3
8	3
9	2
10	2

Rules are similar then by Job Queen, Do Careers and Job Monarch. Why not quadruple your earnings.

⚜ CareersKing

Services Available At CareersKing:

Employment Agencies post your job postings and/or Resumes from your Jobseekers and/or Employers for Free. You won't pay a dime until you get results. Every contact made either from Jobseeker or Employer to one of your listings will cost you a dollar ($1.00).

Employers can post job postings at very affordable prices sometimes mores than 70% lower than at the competition.

Job Search for a permanent or contract position by keyword, job title, skills, state, city or area code.

Use **My CareersKing** Create a personalized My CareersKing account today and get all the tools needed to find your next position. It's free and simple! Once you register you'll have access to these powerful career-enhancing tools.

Post Your Resume CareersKing has a lot of employers seeking quality Tech Professionals like you. It only takes a few simple steps and your online resume is ready!

Confidential Profile Our new passive candidate database is also a great way to test the waters if you are willing to look at the right offer. Our confidential profile allows you to be contacted without revealing your contact information or resume.

Job Alert Just enter the job criteria you're looking for and receive daily e-mails when a new position is posted on CareersKing. You can create up to 5 email search agents!

Career Resources This is a great place to find relevant career-related information. Spruce up your resume, join an association or user group, discover a new programming resource, learn about going independent and more.

Private & Confidential The information you provide to CareersKing stays here at CareersKing. We understand privacy is a concern, and we do not resell any of our user information. You can rest assured that your personal information, background and skills are for CareersKing's hiring customers only.

Affiliate Program offers 10 levels of earning. As a recruiter you can refer other affiliates and earn commission. You get commission from every job seeker, staffing agency/employment agency or employer you refer, and from every job

www.CareersKing.com

Reporter, Editor, Sales Rep, Innovator or Manager

Planet Informer is offering amazing opportunities all over the World. Aspiring Reporters who wants to get some attention, they have perfect opportunity to do so at Planet Informer. Planet Informer covers over 500 biggest cities in the world. Sales Reps who want to try something new, they can offer their Clients perfect Advertising Solution.

Manager of one of city newspaper has plenty of work to do, but also amazing potential to do something with city newspaper. There are two kind of Managers for each city newspaper. Newspaper Manager and small classifieds newspaper Manager.

As a Manager of the city Newspaper you have a chance to build it up as you wish, accepting requirements of the Company but with a lot of personal freedom. Forming a team is not an easy job, but when you are done, you have secure well paid job for times to come.

If you have any service to offer which could benefit you and Planet Informer they'll review your offer and get back to you.

3.

Payment processing - Auctions

CosmoPal.com is offering unique way of Auctions where you actually can put all stuff from your store in and use CosmoPal.com also as a payment processor. It's a perfect solution for someone who has off and online store.

If you own a store and except the credit cards you would be able to offer your merchandise in Auctions and be a Payment Processor.

www.CosmoPal.com

4.

International Payment Processing and Sales

PayNice.com offers many simple business opportunities and International Payment Exchange Processing. You can be anywhere in the world, if you can handle area you applied for, you can be an Exchange Payment Processor for PayNice.com.

What is an Exchange Processor?

An Exchange Processor provide service to people from particular Area who want to deposit some Money in their online Accounts. Let say you are located in China or India and some people want to make a deposit. They'll pay you with cash, money order, local card or any other kind of payment accepted in that area and you'll deposit it to their account for a fee 3 - 5%. You need an Exchange Processor Account which you'll get after your application is approved. Let say person want to deposit $100.00 in PayNice.com online Account. This person will pay you a $100.00 plus all Exchange and processing fees. You'll wire the payment with other payments to PayNice.com and when you get credit in your online PayNice.com Account than you transfer to each person required amount. When you have a lot of transactions and permanent deposit at your online Account you can do that as soon as you see that the payment was confirmed from the person who is paying you. So you transfer the Money to that person account as soon as you see confirmation. You can do that with proven clients with solid history.

[_____] [Search]

Welcome

PayNice members

[▶ LOG IN]

New user?

[▶ SIGN UP]

- Do business as yourself, under a corporate name, or group name
- Payment Receiving Preferences
- Subscriptions
- Mass Payments
- Multi-User Access
- Advanced Downloadable logs
- Send Money
- Request Money
- Website Payments

Corporate   Accounts   Fees   Privacy   Security   Contact Us   User Agreement   Developers   Referrals   Mass Pay   Exchange Providers   Partners

www.PayNice.com

5.

Students' rock

Students Globe (acquired by dequba.com) gives you incredible possibilities selling and buying stuff first hand without commission and even make money. This kind of business is especially interesting for students who want to try their business skills and start their own business without risking a dime. You can take over portal for city or college; organize a team who will manage different categories and dealing with sales and advertising.

6.

Models, Performers and Actors

DeQuba Portfolio service offers tools to sale your songs, print photos and your services online.

www.FerkEnterprises.com

7.

Whole life is a gamble; give the People what they want

PoseidonsPoker.com, NeptunPoker.com and other gives
you a chance to get your share of gambling money. If you
want to own a Poker site and a license for no down
payment you should try them. You could easy make
couple of hundred if not couple of thousand per day.

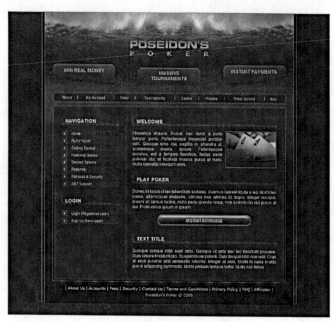

www.PoseidonsPoker.com

8.

Xhq6.com helps you to put your project on the Net

IT Engineers, programmers, System Analysts are bidding for projects.

9.

For IT specialists only ...

Yuxor.com is open project which gives IT Specialists Opportunity to get a share of wealth in software development.

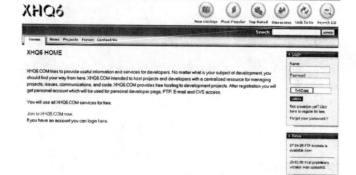

10.

Take a piece of pie from future giant

Cararu.com – take a chance and become a coworker. Will it be a future giant or not? Who knows? There are all predispositions for Cararu to grow and develop real big. The concept, offer and Companies standing behind are promising a lot. You can try with it and see where it goes. If people would know what will happen to Google, Yahoo, Overture(former GoTo) they would stick by them from the beginning.

You can (will be able to) participate in Cararu development through 6netave.com. 6netave.com will be leading the Campaign, Affiliate program and PR.

If you want to promote your web site for no money down or little money down, you should definitely use Cararu.com.

B2B Corporate Submit URL

Advertising Auctions Classifieds Directory Entertainment Employment Press Releases Recent Searches

Cararu © 2003 - 2007

www.Cararu.com

11.

Messenger and Browser which brings cash

Ougo.com is a goose with the golden eggs. You can promote your pages promoting ougo.com. For every free download you'll get certain amount of impressions for your page. You can see reward structure at ougo.com. There are also few open posts for Sales Reps.

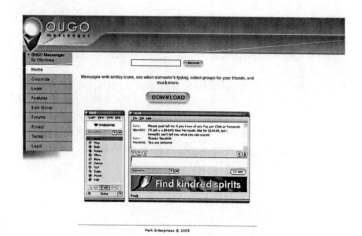

www.Ougo.com

12.

Advertising, PR & Marketing

They'll give you a chance with fresh ideas and you can make your first million. Advivid.com is the right place for dynamic people. You can find all kind of Advertising and all kind of openings for free position in Advertising Business. This Company doesn't care from which part of the world are you and what is your Education, if you are good, job is yours.

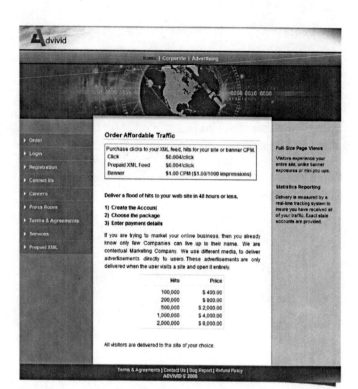

- Order
- Login
- Registration
- Contact Us
- Careers
- Press Room
- Terms & Agreements
- Services
- Prepaid XML

Order Affordable Traffic

Purchase clicks to your XML feed, hits for your site or banner CPM.

Click	$0.004/click
Prepaid XML Feed	$0.004/click
Banner	$1.00 CPM ($1.00/1000 impressions)

Deliver a flood of hits to your web site in 48 hours or less.

1) Create the Account
2) Choose the package
3) Enter payment details

If you are trying to market your online business, then you already know only few Companies can live up to their name. We are contextual Marketing Company. We use different media, to deliver advertisements directly to users. These advertisements are only delivered when the user visits a site and open it entirely.

Hits	Price
100,000	$ 400.00
200,000	$ 800.00
500,000	$ 2,000.00
1,000,000	$ 4,000.00
2,000,000	$ 8,000.00

All visitors are delivered to the site of your choice.

Full Size Page Views

Visitors experience your entire site, unlike banner exposures or maxi pop ups.

Statistics Reporting

Delivery is measured by a real-time tracking system to insure you have received all of your traffic. Exact stats accounts are provided.

www.Advivid.com

13.

Investors and investor hunters

Hotvivid.com is the place for investors and investor hunters. You can start with no money down, with 20 grants or with few hundred thousand dollars. Every category will give you fair start depends on how high you can go Financially.

www.Hotvivid.com

14.

Forums are the key

Qyao.com is forum where you can open any kind of discussion which must be of course legal and moral. What ever you are doing, especially if you are dealing with people, you should consider meetings or at least meetings in forum. As long as you meet with people motivate and encourage them on daily or at least weekly basis, they might perform and deliver results.

QYAO
qyao.com

[Search]

◉ Web ○ Newsgroups ○ Personals ○ Jobs ○ Portfolios ○ Auctions ○ Directory

More Places

www.Qyao.com

15.

Pay Per Click Search Engines

It's not as easy as it looks. Pay Per Click Search Engines starting out in 1998 when grand daddy of them all www.overture.com former www.goto.com started, were simpler than today. Now every average PPC SE needs whole bunch of filters and controls.

What is Pay Per Click Search Engine?

Search engine where results are ranked according to the bid amount, and advertisers are charged when a searcher clicks on the search listing. A search engine in which the ranking of your site is determined by the amount you are paying for each click from that search engine to your site. Examples of pay per click search engines are 7uw.com, Dasington.com, etc. A search engine where the results are composed of advertisers who pay a fee for each click on their listing. The advertiser willing to pay the most is ranked highest. A search engine where advertisers bid for placement.

www.7UW.com

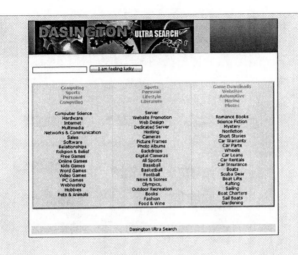

DASINGTON ULTRA SEARCH

[   ] [I am feeling lucky]

Computing	Sports	Game Downloads
Sports	Personal	Websites
Personal	Lifestyle	Automotive
Computing	Literature	Marine
		Photos

	Server	Romance Books
Computer Science	Website Promotion	Science Fiction
Hardware	Web Design	Mystery
Internet	Dedicated Server	Nonfiction
Multimedia	Hosting	Short Stories
Networks & Communication	Cameras	Car Warranty
Sales	Picture Frames	Car Parts
Software	Photo Albums	Wheels
Relationships	Backdrops	Car Loans
Religion & Belief	Digital Cameras	Car Rentals
Free Games	All Sports	Car Insurance
Online Games	Baseball	Boats
Kids Games	Basketball	Scuba Gear
Word Games	Football	Boat Lifts
Video Games	News & Scores	Rafting
PC Games	Olympics,	Sailing
Webhosting	Outdoor Recreation	Boat Charters
Hobbies	Books	Sail Boats
Pets & Animals	Fashion	Gardening
	Food & Wine	

Dasington Ultra Search

www.Dasington.com

COCKTA
International Real Estate

International Real Estate

Search [   ] ●

● FAQ
● Terms & Conditions
● Privacy
Support email
● info@Cockta.com

Home
Home improvement, Cooking, Alarm Systems

Online education
Education, Distance Learning, MBA

Shopping
Discount flower, Flower delivery, Tropical flower

Entertainment
Corporate entertainment, Reno entertainment, Adult entertainment

Insurance
Travel insurance, Health insurance quote, Health insurance

Travel
Europe travel, Business travel, Travel trailer

Lifestyle
Food and Wine, Astrology, Children

Gift
Holiday gift, Baby gift, Personalized gift

Web & E-Commerce
Paid Email, Online Trading, Web Traffic

Nutrition
Weight loss pill, Enzymes, Sports nutrition

Services
Marketing service, Internet service, Financial service

Legal
Divorce, Divorce, Surveillance

Internet
Ecommerce web hosting, Web hosting service, Affiliate marketing

Electronics
Cellular accessory, Xcr dvd, Cordless phone

Gambling
Nevada casino, Roulette online, Home loan

Partners

www.Cockta.com

Search Engine Terms

Alt Tag: The alternative text that the browser displays when the surfer does not want to or cannot see the pictures present in a web page. Using alt tags containing keywords can improve the search engine ranking of the page for those keywords.

Click Popularity: A measure of the relevance of sites obtained by noting which sites are clicked on most and how much time users spend in each site. Click through - The process of clicking on a link in a search engine results page to visit an indexed site.

Click through rate (CTR) - The ratio of clicks and display impressions of an ad. If an ad were displayed 100 times and 4 viewers clicked on it, you have a CTR of 4%. Comment - The HTML tags are used to hide text from browsers. Some search engines ignore text between these symbols but others index such text as if the comment tags were not there. The text present within the tags in a web page. Most search engines will ignore the text within the Comment Tags.

Cloaking: The process by which your site can display different pages under different circumstances. It is primarily used to show an optimized page to the search engines and a different page to humans. Most search engines will penalize a site if they discover that it is using cloaking.

Crawlers - Also know as a "robot" or "spider", a crawler is an automated software program that runs at many search engines, reads sites' content, analyzes it, and inserts them into the index (or collects information for later insertion into the index).

Description tag - HTML tag used to by Web page authors to provide a description for search engine listings. Some engines display these descriptions, other display some text from your page containing the searched phrase.
Directories - A directory is a web site, which contains listings (usually searchable and categorized) of other web sites. Most directories are created and managed by human editors.

Doorway page - A page which has been specially created in order to get a high ranking in the search engines. Also called gateway page, bridge page, entry page etc. Any page through which a visitor can enter your site. Some people prepare special pages to rank well in search engines for particular keywords, serving as an entry point through which visitors pass to the main content.

Dynamic Content: Information in web pages which changes automatically, based on database or user information. Search engines will index dynamic content in the same way as static content unless the URL includes a ? mark. However, if the URL does include a ? mark, many search engines will ignore the URL.

Entry Page: See Doorway Page.

Frames: An HTML technique allowing web site designers to display two or more pages in the same browser window. Many search engines do not index framed web pages properly - they only index the text present in the NOFRAMES tag. Unless a web page which uses frames contains relevant content in the NOFRAMES tag, it is unlikely to get a high ranking in those search engines.

Gateway Page: See Doorway Page.

Hallway Page: A page containing links to various doorway pages.

Heading Tags: A paragraph style that is displayed in a large, bold typeface. Having text containing keywords in the Heading Tags can improve the search engine ranking of a page for those keywords.

Hidden Text: Text that is visible to the search engines but is invisible to humans. It is mainly accomplished by using text in the same color as the background color of the page. It is primarily used for the purpose of including extra keywords in the page without distorting the aesthetics of the page. Most search engines penalize web sites which use such hidden text.

Image Map: An image containing one or more invisible regions which are linked to other pages. If the image map is defined as a separate file, the search engines may not be able to index the pages to which that image map links. The way out is to have text hyperlinks to those pages in addition to the links from the image map. However, image maps defined within the same web page will generally not prevent search engines from indexing the other pages. Keyword - A word used in a performing a search. Generally visitors search for phrases instead of single words to locate the required information. Keyword Density - A measure of how frequently a given keyword appears within a given web page.

Keyword marketing - Putting your message in front of people who are searching using particular keywords and key phrases. Keyword Phrase - A phrase, which forms (part of) a search engine query. Keyword Purchasing - The buying of search keywords from search engines, usually to control banner ad or Pay-per-click advertising.

Keyword research - The search for keywords related to your Web site, and the analysis of which ones yield the highest return on investment (ROI). Keywords tag - META tag used to help define the primary keywords of a Web page. Link popularity - A measure of the quantity and quality of sites that link to your site.

Link text - The text contained in (and sometimes near) a hyperlink.

Log file - File that records the activity on a Web server.

Manual submission - Adding a URL to the search engines individually by hand.

Meta Tags - Meta Tags are HTML elements that can optionally be included within web pages, and contain information about the document such as the author, keywords describing the document, a description of the document, etc.

JavaScript: A scripting language commonly used in web pages. Most search engines are unable to index these scripts properly.

Keyword: A word or phrase that you type in when you are searching for information in the search engines.

Keyword Frequency: Denotes how often a keyword appears in a page or in an area of a page. In general, higher the number of times a keyword appears in a page, higher its search engine ranking. However, repeating a keyword too often in a page can lead to that page being penalized for spamming.

Keyword Prominence: Denotes how close to the start of an area of a page that a keyword appears. In general, having the keyword closer to the start of an area will lead to an improvement in the search engine ranking of a page.

Keyword Weight: Denotes the number of times a keyword appears in a page as a percentage of all the other words

in the page. In general, higher the weight of a particular keyword in a page, higher will be the search engine ranking of the page
for that keyword. However, repeating a keyword too often in order to increase its weight can cause the page to be penalized by the search engines.

Link Popularity: The number of sites which link to a particular site. Many search engines use link popularity as a factor in determining the search engine ranking of a web site.

Meta Description Tag: The tag present in the header of a web page which is used to provide a short description of the contents of the page. Some search engines will display the text present in the Meta Description Tag when the page appears in the results of a search. Including keywords in the Meta Description Tag can improve the search engine ranking of a page for those keywords. However, some search engines ignore the Meta Description Tag.

Meta Keywords Tag: The tag present in the header of a web page which is used to provide alternative words for the words used in the body of the page. The Meta Keywords Tag is becoming less and less important in influencing the search engine ranking of a page. Some search engines ignore the Meta Keywords tag.

Meta Refresh Tag: The tag present in the header of a web page which is used to display a different page after a few seconds. If a page displays another page too soon, most search engines will either ignore the current page and index the second page or penalize the current page for spamming.

Pay Per Click Search Engine: A search engine in which the ranking of your site is determined by the amount you are paying for each click from that search engine to your site. Examples of pay per click search engines are 6netave, Stonediver etc.

Search engine where results are ranked according to the bid amount, and advertisers are charged when a searcher clicks on the search listing.

Pay per inclusion search engine - Search engine where web sites or certain pages are included in the index only when you pay them a fee. The rank is not guaranteed and is based on the engines ranking algorithm or rules. Positioning- The process of ordering web sites or web pages by a search engine or a directory so that the most relevant sites appear first in the search results for a particular query.

Positioning Technique - A method of modifying a web page so that search engines (or a particular search engine) treat the page as more relevant to a particular query (or a set of queries).

Query - A word, a phrase or a group of words, possibly combined with other syntax used to pass instructions to a search engine or a directory in order to locate web pages.

Rank - The position a particular site is listed in a search engine after a person does a relevant search. The higher the rank, the nearer the top of the results the site will come, and usually, the more traffic it will get.

Registration - The process of informing a search engine or directory that a new web page or web site should be indexed.

Re-submission - Repeating the search engine registration process one or more times for the same page or site. Generally it is unnecessary to do this with spider based search engines.

Robots - Also know as a "crawler" or "spider", a robot is an automated software program that runs at many search engines, reads sites' content, analyzes it, and inserts them into the index (or collects information for later insertion into theindex).

Robot: In the context of search engine ranking, it implies the same thing as Spider. In a different context, it is also used to indicate a software which visits web sites and collects email addresses to be used for sending unsolicited bulk email.

Robots.txt: A text file present in the root directory of a site which is used to control which pages are indexed by a robot. Only robots which comply with the Robots Exclusion Standard will follow the instructions contained in this file.

Search Engine: A software that searches for information and returns sites which provide that information. Examples of search engines are AltaVista, Google, Hotbot etc.

Search Engine Placement: The practice of trying to ensure that a web site obtains a high rank in the search engines. Also called search engine positioning, search engine optimization etc.

Spamming: Using any search engine ranking technique which causes a degradation in the quality of the results produced by the search engines. Examples of spamming include excessive repetition of a keyword in a page, optimizing a page for a keyword which is unrelated to the contents of the site, using invisible text, etc. Most search engines will penalize a page which uses spamming. In a different context, spamming is also used to mean the practice of sending unsolicited bulk email.

Spider: A software that visits web sites and indexes the pages present in those sites. Search engines use spiders to build up their databases. Example: The spider for AltaVista is called Scooter.

Search Engine Optimization (SEO) - The art of optimizing a site to generate traffic from search engines.

Search engine submission - The act of supplying a URL to a search engine in an attempt to make a search engine aware of a site or page. Submission Service - Any agent, which submits your site to many search engines and directories.

Title tag - HTML tag used to define the text in the top line of a Web browser, also used by many search engines as the title of search listings.

Top 20 - The top twenty search engine results for a particular search term.

Traffic - The visitors to a web page or web site. Also refers to the number of visitors, hits, accesses etc. over a given period.

URL - Uniform Resource Locator - Location of a resource on the Internet.

Title Tag: The contents of the Title tag is generally displayed by the browser at the top of the browser window. The search engines use the Title tag to provide a link to the sites which match the query made by the user. Having keywords in the Title tag of a page can significantly increase the search engine ranking of the page for those keywords.

Volunteer directory - A Web directory staffed primarily by unpaid volunteer editors.

Billions with Search Engines

How Search Engines Work

Score in Search Engine Result Pages is very important for online business and if your page isn't reaching first page or at least first three pages, you might be doing something wrong.

Understanding how search engines operate will help you understand what can go wrong.

All search engines perform the following four tasks:

Web crawling. Search engines send out automated programs, sometimes called "bots" or "spiders," which use the web's hyperlink structure to "crawl" its pages. According to some of our best estimates, search engine spiders have crawled maybe half of the pages that exist on the Internet.

Indexing. After spiders crawl a page, its content needs to be put into a format that makes it easy to retrieve when a user queries the search engine. Thus, pages are stored in a huge, tightly managed database that makes up the search engine's index. These indexes contain billions of documents, which are delivered to users in mere fractions of a second.

Queries. When a user queries a search engine, which happens hundreds of millions of times each day, the engine examines its index to find documents that match. Queries that look superficially the same can yield very different results. For example, searching for the phrase "all newspapers in Europe," yields more than four million results in bigger Search Engines. Add a word or "!" and you'll get totally different result.

Ranking. Search Engine isn't going to show you all results on the same page – and even if it did, it needs some way to decide which ones should show up first. Thus, the search engine runs an algorithm on the results to calculate which ones are most relevant to the query. These are shown first, with all the others in descending order of relevance. If you are selling some content and charge people for that, you don't want Search Engines spiders to index that page and show it for free to people. Of course there are ways to deliberately block indexing of those pages.

Very effective blocker for spiders are Dynamic URLs, those are URL's which change depending on visitors content. Visitor has to put in some parameters and some info to get those pages for example a zip code, birth date, etc.

Pages that are more than three clicks from website's home page also might not be crawled. Spiders don't like to go that deep. Many humans can get lost on a website with that many levels of links if there isn't some kind of navigational help.

Pages requiring a "Session ID" or cookie for navigation also might not be spidered. Spiders don't have the same capabilities as browsers. Another spider block is pages in frames. Many web designers like frames to keep page navigation in one place even when a user scrolls through content. Pages with frames confusing to spiders.

Pages with hundreds of unique links are also turn off for spiders. There are different ways to organize your Site Map. Spiders don't like pages which can be accessed only after filling out a form and hitting "Submit" or pages that require use of a drop down menu to access might not be spidered, and the same for documents that can only be accessed via a search box.

Documents blocked will most likely not be spidered and you can handle this with a robots meta tag or robots.txt file. Pages that require a login block search engine spiders. Invite spiders to index your pages. They'll start at your home page and follow the links which are at your home page. If you don't have a link to particular site you want them to spider they most likely won't see it. Keep the links as simple and asclear as possible.

How PPC SE's work

PPC SE signs for Xml feed by some other bigger PPC SE or regular SE. Results from bigger Partner are shown in this smaller PPC SE. Affiliates from PPC SE come and click on these result, of course they click on results because they are paid for clicking.

After a while Advertisers get upset because there is no conversion and they leave or complaint first and than leave. Bigger partners have to react officially and discipline smaller PPC SE's which were allow till this moment to send trashy traffic.

Bigger Partners Terminates Accounts from those who are new, to small and/or send to trashy traffic. That's how they deal with traffic quality. Of course they don't pay smaller partners for traffic sent in last 3 – 4 months. Usually most of them pay on net 45 and payment always slide for a couple of days or a week.

Pay per Click Search Engine (PPC SE)

How to start Pay per Click Search Engine ?

Find a programmer who will make a code for Pay per click Search Engine(Concept for PPC SE). You can buy really cheap code online for couple of hundred dollars and have instant problems, losing your nerves, time and money. Other solution is to Invest 30,000 or more to one which is already running. You can make with your search engine couple of thousand dollars or couple of millions, it's up to you. If you neglect your business most likely you'll be doing under $10,000.00 per month, but if you dedicate time, educate yourself and start working hard, your PPC SE won't disappoint you.

Remember just be fair, give your Advertisers what you would want if you would advertise in your PPC SE. Best choice and the most affordable one; go to hotvivid.com and buy new fresh PPC SE with know how and start producing couple of thousands of profit from the first month. First you must be clear what you want from your Pay per click Search Engine.

You must decide would you like classic pay per click Search Engine where customers bid for rankings in your listings. Would you like to have only Search Engine where will be listed results from other Search Engines which has own live advertisers. Search Engine where customers won't bid for listings but they'll pay average same rate for listing. Search Engine where listings will be free except first 3 sponsored Results in the listing   Buy existing code for few hundred dollars There are many scripts you can buy for few dollars on Ebay, but with those scripts you are limited and you don't have any control what are your affiliates doing, you can't block the cheaters, you can't spot the spidering, you are left on mercy of your visitors. With that kind of Search Engine you can forget partnership with other bigger Search Engines because those who are serious won't tolerate such behavior and they'll terminate the contract with you in few days. Get a free code

Free code is even worse. You'll have with all mentioned problems also problem with service. Companies which offers free code without service they have no obligation to service the code. It's a different story if you lease a

Search Engine where the company offers also a service for monthly fee (cymicom.com is one of them but they limited lease of software on Search Engines which are able to send at least 10,000 searches per Day so go check hotvivid.com). Name of Search Engine When you are big already name is not so important, but at start you should choose the name which is associated with search, seek, look, etc. Don't combine that with cash, money, dollars, earn, pay, etc. When people see that they place you in the same category with small opportunity sites witch have mostly lame design and low quality. Design be careful with design. If you want to run serious business you need professional design. It's better spent few hundred bucks more for professional design then later notice people don't take you serious. Hosting When you start you can find yourself a hosting for few dollars per month. You can start already with $ 20.00/ month. That would be 10 Giga of monthly bandwidth and about 500 M space on hard drive. But if you are successful you'll be changing hosting plan very soon and leasing dedicated server for $ 300.00 or more per month.

- P4 1.6 GHz Processor
- With up to 1GB of ram
- Single Hard Drive you'd be doing about 30,000 daily searches and over 7,000 visits
- Clicks on results of your

When you goover that limit you'll be needing more powerful server

- P4 Xeon 2.4 GHz Processors
- with 512K Cache Server Works GC-LE chipset, supporting a 400MHz FSB- Up to 6GB 200MHz DDR SDRAM
- with Advanced ECC & Online Spare Memory capabilities
- 2 Gigabit Ethernet NICs- Up to 6 Hard Drives- hot swappable SCSI

- Embedded Wide Ultra3 Smart Array 5i Plus RAID controller- Supports Raid 0,1,0+1,5,50
- Redundant power supplies
- Redundant fans After that you'll be having own server farm and IT staff ready 24/7.

Affiliate program Very careful with Affiliate program. People are always the most sensitive part. Affiliate program should function most of it automatic.

When Affiliates signup they should first receive confirmation email which they are obligate to confirm before they can enter their account. Affiliate program without that option can cause a lot of problems. There are many people who will try to harm Affiliate program from many reasons and they can sign with someone else email for example admin@policedepartment.com and this email address would be receiving unsolicited emails and owner of Search Engine with that kind of Affiliate program would have a lot of problems explaining that.

Advertisers are the most difficult to get. There is no 100% formula how to get them. But to get them at all you have to prepare your site user friendly, with great design, site where everyone finds everything easy and quick. Serve them first short explanation why they should advertise with you then show them a demo and after that if they want you have to offer them specify explanation about rules, possibilities and benefits they'll get when they sign for advertisement at your page.

Almost all Pay per Click Search Engines are making same mistake, they offer great traffic just first three top advertisers. All others are getting few clicks per day. It's true they all compete for those top 3 positions but take different approach and you'll have hundreds of satisfying customers. Use the rotating system for the same bid value. If bid value at fourth position is $ 0.24 allow 10 advertisers with the same bid to rotate on fourth position.

You will accomplish that every advertiser at fourth position will get more or less same amount of clicks and visitors who search at your Search Engine will get always different sites to review. Also it won't happen that only one

Advertiser will spend his//her money in one day at one position while being alone. Instead of 30 advertisers you can make satisfied 300 advertisers listed at first page and offer instead of 30 results 300 different results listed at first page and they all stay only on 30 positions. With that system you can also offer advertisers 3 Premium listings on position above the line and you list rest of the results beneath the line which will separate regular bided links from premium listings.

Premium listings shouldn't rotate; they have to be only one for each position. Offer your advertisers to show their brand with banners and skyscrapers. Don't use annoying popup ads even if they are transferable and visitors don't know from where and when they came. Sooner or later they'll connect you to those ads. Partners Xml feeds Many Pay per Click Search Engines are offering xml feed – transfer their data and list it as your results. Regular visitor doesn't even notice what is happening at the site. Problem with xml feed is that if partner who gave you xml feed have problems and your tech staff didn't set up the time out for receiving xml feed, your site will be down when ever visitors search for something and none of listings will be displayed. Of course you'll be loosing money.

Also don't show bid value especially if you have affiliates. For regular visitor bid value is sometimes annoying and for affiliate is like a magnet. Affiliate sees opportunity to use highest bided words and Advertisers will be calling you in no time what is that mean that they are receiving visitors just through highest bided links. Many times xml providers – your partners will ask you to filter foreign traffic. This could be time consuming and disturbing for visitors.

While you translating IP's into form where you can see from where is traffic and if you should filter it or not, it takes 3 or more seconds which are annoying for visitor. If you are getting International traffic make sure that your affiliates don't abuse your Search Engine for their own profits. You'll lose partners and advertisers. You'll have to reimburse them and you'll upset affiliates and you'll have a lot of work with all that.

Getting paid be careful how you choose partners who will provide you with xml feed. It doesn't matter from where they are or how big they are, when you become to heavy for them, they'll find a reason not to pay. When you start with new partner let it run low, it's better to lose $1,000.00 then $ 30,000.00 and most of them have payouts net 45 or net 60 business days. That would mean if you start with them on August 1, you'll get paid October 15 – October 31. Some fair partners will only deduct fraudulent amount of money if they spotted fraudulent activities from your affiliates and they'll call you and tell you to take care about it and block the crook.

The other with financial problems will see opportunity to deduct payment and divide it in 2 or 3 payouts and those unprofessional will stop complete payment. Good partners will give you at least 2 options how will they pay you, usually check or wire. Almost all partners do the shaving, they crunch your amount in their statistic and they shaved it even before that. There are many different ways how to do that. They don't count all valid clicks or they set unique IP on 48 hours instead of 24.

When the amount is presented you'll get about 70% - 90% of presented amount, because they calculate risk factor of fraudulent activities from you. Really reliable partners are: overture.com, Searchboss.com,

MyGeek.com, Nbcsearch.com, Netvisibility.com, Findology.com, and Genieknows.com. With those you can count 100% you'll get paid and they'll treat you right. Also OK and good are 7search.com, Miva.com, Search123.com, SearchFeed.com and GoClick.com, but if you have problem with your affiliates they'll give you really hard time and you'll be blamed for your sloppy work not monitoring your traffic, usually they'll terminate an agreement, but they'll still pay you for your clean traffic.

If you made a mistake, discuss it with your partners, ask for help and advice but don't cover it up it's the worse you can do. Almost all of them will be happy to help you because they don't like to lose source of traffic and you can learn from them. Pay Affiliates Treat your affiliates correct. Don't relay just on one source of traffic, reward affiliates for referrals, set them straight from the beginning and tell them what they are allowed and what they shouldn't do. Help them and you'll benefit from that but don't let them rule or force you to do something what they want just they wouldn't leave. Set the payment by %and date so that you will be able to pay in time and in full. Try not to shave, because everybody does and you can benefit from that if other hear you are fair. Set the system so that you approve the site before they can start sending you traffic. You must see every site and try it out before you approve it.

Check Alexa rating (alexa.com) and if they are sending high amount of traffic and rating is low something is wrong unless if they provide others with own xml feed where yours is included. Small affiliates who has search box at their site are usually sending few searches per day. If you notice searches are increasing and decreasing ask them why and they should give you reasonable explanation.

Require from them all data if data is incomplete freeze them account and tell them why. Most of affiliates open more accounts under different names and they don't list any addresses, they just list Paypal email and ask you to pay with Paypal.

They usually set spidering scripts on low and middle value bids and send for maybe $ 0.60 - $ 1.40 daily searches per account, they open of course 30 or more accounts on different names and when is payout they just change Paypal emails and you'll see one Paypal email in more accounts. If not sooner then you must terminate their accounts immediately without any payment. Such fraudulent activities can cost you few solid business partners and advertisers and other will avoid your Search Engine.

Some scripts are very difficult to spot. You must know that those guys who write that scripts and sell them (Russians and Chinese programmers mostly) they are very good in writing those scripts but they don't know the system. Automatic filters doesn't spot those scripts, also your partners doesn't spot them and everything seems to be fine, but advertisers start complaining about ROI and then you have major problem. Nothing can save you.

You can have perfect traffic and a lot of it but when advertisers start complaining about you, you are dead meat by Advertisers and by partners. But here is one way how to recognize those accounts which are sending you traffic with scripts. The best way is to explain that with example:

Few German students from Aachen and Munich bought a Russian script for $99.00. They opened 30 accounts or more at few different smaller Search Engines clones with poor script and limited features bought from Company which never run own Search Engine.

Owners of smaller Search Engine noticed traffic increment but traffic was fine different IP's, unique clicks and everything was so perfect so they didn't even bother to investigate any further. If they would take a look they would see that every click was unique time stamp was 1 – 3 sec and each IP was different. IP's were all American IP's, but after a month and a half problems just started. They paid those students and after that they lost partners and of course their business. Control bigger affiliates even more you have to control bigger affiliates and their traffic. Track them through secondary ID or so named sub ID. Because they can hurt you even more.

There are many ways how to check traffic from your affiliates without offending or harming anyone. The best way is to cooperate with them and ask them for feedback and also ask them to include secondary/sub ID to their affiliates. Be fair, pay on time and stimulate them with bigger revenue share. Ask them where they advertise and if they have traffic outbursts why they have them.

The best method and best approach has Ah-ha.com. They control their affiliates and they always call them and discus with them problems and they try to help them. Contests It's smart to make contests and keep affiliates on their toes. With contests Search Engine gain a lot of new referrals, more traffic and more promotion for low cost.

Let's say Search Engine offers a reward $ 10,000 per day to random user. This is not a bad incentive because users will come to Search Engine which is offering contest while they searching for something. They'll go to other big Search Engines and directories as usual but they'll also come to your Search Engine. It's different from affiliates who usually click for money and they know more clicks they make more money they get. It's OK for them and it's OK for you only as long as it's fair clean real traffic to Advertisers. With contest they'll use your Search Engine only for real stuff. Of course contest must be set up so that they don't need to click more then one time. You get a lot of free and quality traffic and you make more money.

Advertisers are satisfied and they are keep coming back. Spam Usually happen when affiliates want to increase the traffic and they start using email services which are sending bulk email to "known" users. Those "known" users get upset because of unsolicited emails and you get your share of trouble. Scam/Cheating This happen mostly by smaller affiliates who don't have enough money for advertising or they just want easier way. They usually send scripts over different results.

Most of scripts are so advanced that filter from (also the biggest) Search Engines doesn't recognize them. To staff who should control that traffic looks fine. Many times happened that big boys try their shoot in the dark. By those who they assume is something what they can't explain they terminate affiliate accounts. Sometimes is the reason just financial trouble. Search Engine which gives xml feed to other Search Engine many times, when it's about bigger payouts, just accuse other party of cheating. In best case scenario they pay 40% to 60% in rates of 2 – 3 months.

Worse case scenario if they pay on net 45 and they don't pay at all at the end. Also big boys play sometimes dirty. It doesn't matter how much traffic you have, don't let more traffic to any partner then for $ 5,000.00 to $ 9,000.00 or risk you won't get paid one day. Proxy Spidering scripts are running usually over proxies, but more advanced programmers will use real US IP's in their scripts and even take care about time stamp. Most of the time they made mistake because they become to greedy.

Proxies are not necessary reason for alarm, many people use them and not all with bad intentions. Proxies are hard to control and paid proxies are listed much later when commissions for traffic were already paid.

Also you can check proxies by some sites but you can control them at least not them all. You sure can see a lot what is happening if you have data base of proxies, but a lot of them you can't spot at the right time.Kanoodle.com successfully practiced filtering through proxies.

Spidering

Spidering script has similar effect then script for check broken links at your page with only difference that by spidering script IP's are changing and script match search and clicks with same IP. Automatic filter can be set on counter if there is more then 9 different IP's from 10 selected IP's on same affiliate ID or secondary/sub ID then account must be blocked automatically. But this works only at smaller accounts. By bigger accounts can that happened and none of spidering scripts will be involved and you'll be doing injustice to your affiliates. Only thing which shows almost for sure is time stamp.

Time stamp (spidering and/or Opera –shift multiple clicks) Sometimes happen that some of your users search with old Opera browser and press shift and open sites more windows the same effect is also in Explorer with open more windows. User who opened more windows will open different sites in those windows with 1 or 2 seconds different time stamp. What is certainly alarm for your partners tech staff. But when you see time stamp or 1 sec then you can be sure it's spidering script.

Problem of big ISP providers (more affiliates on one IP) It's not an actual problem. For example more AOL users are on same IP and when they are your affiliates they won't be for long, because they won't be able to produce for you any revenue or at least not much revenue.

Advertisers will see most of the time repeated clicks from same IP, they won't know the traffic is ok

Traffic from forbidden countries

This could be a real problem specially for Search Engines with Affiliate programs with insufficient filters. USA Advertisers are not happy with non USA traffic as European Advertisers aren't happy with non European traffic and of course both aren't happy with Asian or African traffic. Each Advertiser yearn for traffic from area where it operates, sale products or services. Not many Advertisers advertise globally.

The main problem isn't from where traffic come but why it comes. It's still better to have a buyer from Shanghai or Morocco then affiliate from Toronto with incentive clicks. As long as traffic brings buyers it doesn't matter from where it comes. Children safe environment Take care your Search Engine is children safe environment. Place filters on. Be careful that you don't show adult sites to kids. It's not just illegal it's also immoral. You wouldn't expose your kids to adult, violent and other graphic disturbing content, so don't do that to others. Filter for that site is easy, you just block all results which brings sites with included keywords and everything is fine.

Rotating bid system Rotating system (Stonediver.com) really helps equalize amount of Traffic you are sending to your advertisers. On short time you won't be doing so much but on long run more Advertisers will come to you. If you rotate 10 URL's on position with same bid you'll be displaying on first side with 30 results in list up to 300 Advertisers, if you don't rotate results you'll be displaying only 30 Advertisers.

The problem is that rest of 270 advertisers will because of to high biding go to other Search Engines where they have more chances to get visitors for lower price. If we make an example with 9,000 visitors in rotating system first 3 positions with 10 advertiser each will getting 3000 visitors each, which means each advertiser will get about 300 visitors. In regular system first 3positions which are also first 3 advertisers will get 3000 visitors.

In short term you'll be loosing because bids will stay lower at your Search Engine then at others with regular systems but in long run Advertisers will rather advertise with you because they'll get more visitors for more affordable price. The problem with big Search Engines is if you advertise with low bid you won't be getting much traffic and it doesn't matter if they have solid Alexa.com ranking under 3,000 , 1,000 or even lower, because mostly first 3 results are displayed in other Search Engines and other sites through xml feed. It can happen you pay in some Search Engines 30 or more cents per bid and it will take forever to burn out your deposit with visitors. With other search engine you'll pay 10 – 15 % and you'll burnout your deposit very quick with visitors sent to your page.

www.Stonediver.com

Ranking system

Ranking system is very important and you can't satisfy everyone. Most of Search Engines use ranking by higher bid which was first used byOverture.com (former GoTo.com). That kind of ranking system make most of the profit for Search Engine owners what is also the point. Advertisers compete in bidding for higher position and automatic systems for automatic bidding help them. In a lot of Search Engines you can set up automatic bidding system which bids always one cent higher then competition does but not over the limit you set up.

System also lowers bids but also not under a limit which is set by Search Engines and it is between 1 cent and 10cents. Banner Advertise with banner pays off only if Advertiser wants people to see the brand of the company, product or service. Usually price is from $ 1.00 - $35.00 CPM; 1000 impressions per $ 1.00 - $ 35.00. $ 35.00 CPM require sites which are really powerful. They usually charge between $ 12.00 and $35.00 per 1000 impressions. Smaller sites charge under $ 12.00 per 1000impressions. It pays out only to advertise brand this way, because revenue is very low and usually click through ratio is lower then 0.6 %.

Buttons

Buttons are usually placed at front entry page and are charged with flat fee per time period for a week or a month.

Skyscrapers

Skyscrapers are vertical banners and rule is pretty much the same as for horizontal banners.

Popups

Popups are used from sites which
are providing some content for free and you occasional
need it like road maps, weather, news, free email, etc.
Those sites can afford to use them because they are very
annoying to visitors and they are real repellant for visitors.
Popup is site open in usually smaller window which pops
up when you visit or leave the site. Try advivid.com they
offer hits to the site and site isn't open in popup or
popunder.

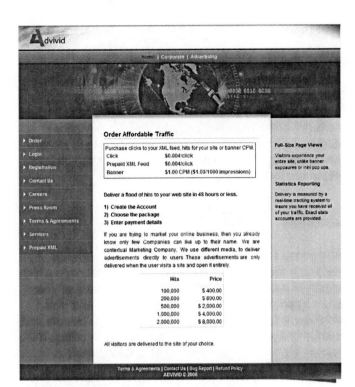

Order Affordable Traffic

Purchase clicks to your XML feed, hits for your site or banner CPM.

Click	$0.004/click
Prepaid XML Feed	$0.004/click
Banner	$1.00 CPM ($1.00/1000 impressions)

Full-Size Page Views

Visitors experience your entire site, unlike banner exposures or mini pop ups.

Statistics Reporting

Delivery is measured by a real-time tracking system to insure you have received all of your traffic. Exact stats accounts are provided.

Deliver a flood of hits to your web site in 48 hours or less.

1) Create the Account
2) Choose the package
3) Enter payment details

If you are trying to market your online business, then you already know only few Companies can live up to their name. We are contextual Marketing Company. We use different media, to deliver advertisements directly to users. These advertisements are only delivered when the user visits a site and open it entirely.

Hits	Price
100,000	$ 400.00
200,000	$ 800.00
500,000	$ 2,000.00
1,000,000	$ 4,000.00
2,000,000	$ 8,000.00

All visitors are delivered to the site of your choice.

www.Advivid.com

Popunders

Popunders are the same with only difference from popups that Popunders opens in background. They are a little bit less annoying then popups but still they work better because visitor is not directly affected and it sees it when he is done with browsing of other sites. Then visitor decide if it is any of his/her interest and close it. More annoying are of course popups which might pop up from popunder by closing it.

404 pages

404 pages are more discreet because they show up when the link is broken and they seems like regular page which is part of entire site. It's recommended to use it at your site so can you cover a little bit any broken links you don't know for them. Alexa ranking many site owners and company agents go first to Alexa to see your rating. It's known it's not completely relevant, but they can get pretty good idea when they see your ranking. So you can't full anyone with claims you have over 100,000 daily hits if your Alexa ranking is 10,000 or more. If you'd have 100,000 daily hits your Alexa ranking would be 3,000 and less.

Alexa is used just for orientation because it's impossible to establish exact amount of traffic unless you see the site stats measured from site itself. Even more irrelevant and bogus is Google ranking. They rank as they are pleased and that it serves their purposes. There many pages getting over 100,000 hits per day and Google ranked them with 1 or even 0. Google was very valuable a year ago but lately its almost obnoxious how arrogant are some Google services towards, their Affiliates and even Customers.   Offering a co-brand Fees for co-branded site of your Content will depend on a range cofactors, including traffic, number of software libraries and design and translation specifications.

Benefits: They Expand their offerings while maintaining the look and feel of their site. Offer their customers the content of your site as it would be their own. Earn greater revenue from advertising sales.

Create (as desired) a more flattering association with the brand. Co-brand Advertising Generally speaking, Co-Branding partners are responsible for handling their own banner ad delivery. The banner ad code can be included in one of the server-side include components that are supplied by the partner. Because banner ad delivery and hosting are under the control of the Co-Branding partner Business requirements yours main business requirement is that your logo should appear in a box on every page. Don't make that a rule; you might lose many partners this way.

Revenue Increase

You can easily increase your revenue if you select better partners who have higher bids and if you offer advertisers smarter bidding. Automatic bidding is one of the solutions for revenue increment. Advertiser has opportunities to set up automatic bidding where system bid advertisers listing always one bid higher then the competition does. Of course must be upper limit otherwise would bidding go sky high because of competitors.

Traffic increase It's always nice when you see traffic increment but it's also smart to take a look from where it comes from. Sudden traffic increment is usually result of spammer who are running scripts. If some affiliate ID have unusual traffic increment take a look what keywords are used, if IP's are unique (every single one), time stamp and referral.

Targeted Email Campaigns Beware of Targeted Email Campaigns because many of them are just incentive paid emails where members of those paid emails will come and click every day to get one or half of cent. Real targeted email campaigns will allow you to have your text which shouldn't encourage receivers to click on your links for money. There is also difference when you offer your visitors to get paid for clicking if you pay them for each click or if you say that all visitors who uses your search engine might be chosen for a reward which will be known at the end of the week or month. In first case they'll click on as many links as possible and possible on links which are bided higher, when in second case they'll just search at your Search Engine when they need something after they already done it at other Search Engines. Don't offer them data form Google or dmoz directory.

Why would they look at your Search Engine for Google results? Everybody who are listed at Google they are also listed at all other Search Engines. Be different otherwise people won't need your services. Other pay per click Search Engines Advertising in other pay per click Search Engines doesn't really pay off. You'd spend more money then you'll get it in. There is also no absolute guarantee for advertiser the ROI will be delivered. None of Search Engines not even big ones can guarantee that.

They'll send visitors and visitors will go to advertiser's page but it depends from advertiser if his/her services or products will be sold. If Advertiser is not educated on how and what to do or if Advertiser does not want to listen you can't help him/her. Such Advertiser will stay till his deposit disappear and never come back. For such Advertiser no Search Engine is good enough. Advertisers can know only from experiences which Search Engine deliver what.

Pay per Click programs

Pay per click programs pay off only with pay per sale and with impressions (co-brand) program sometimes also with pay per lead program. Pay per click never delivers what is expected. Banner Exchange Banner exchange is only good when it's your own, then you are getting Some free traffic. Click through rate is less then 1% and it's also better If you use it for co-brand.   Forums If you don't have your own forum choose one public forum where you'll give advice to your affiliates and of course explain to them what they are allowed and not allowed to do. So you can avoid many misunderstandings and anger. Directory, PPC SE and Basic If you are able to offer your visitors directory PPC SE and basic free listings that would be best. Visitors have a choice and they'd rather come back
to you where they can choose then somewhere else where they get the same results as in any other major Search Engine.

ROI – return on Investment The hardest is to deliver ROI at least to deliver good ROI. Where you See messages how they deliver ROI and how people make sales – forget about it. Test it first with small amount. Some smaller Search Engines allow you to test it for free to amount up to % 5.00 or $ 10.00.

Sometimes you'd be surprised what small Search Engine can deliver. They might have just what you are looking for and send you more then some big Search Engines can. Merchant Account If you want to accept Credit Cards and online payments you'd need Merchant Account especially if you don't use third party for charges. 3rd party online charge 3rd party online charge usually charge you commission from 5.5% up to 11% or even more. SSN/Tax You have to require SSN or Tax ID from your affiliates if you pay them Out more then $ 600.00 per year W9

Form Best way to get their SSN or EIN is to send them W9 form or ask them to download it from the internet Copyrights Be very careful about copyrights and think twice before you use something which can be infringement. Trade Marks always ask companies with registered Trade Marks before you use their logo.

Patents

The same is with patents be sure your system is unique so nobody can sue you for copying.

Privacy

You have to have Privacy Terms at your page, the best way to do it is to check professional sites which will provide you with advice what is the best way to do it.

Terms

You have to have Terms of Services where you explain your visitors, partners and affiliates what kind of system you have and what kind of business you are running.

FAQ

Prepare also Frequently Asked Questions so your visitors will have all explained and will easier decide to participate or at least visit your site more frequently.

Advertising

Be careful how you advertise. Test all media what you think it could work out good for you with smaller advertisements.

Newspapers

Newspapers are not a good choice to advertise your Search Engine unless you are making more then a million per month.

Magazines

Magazines are also not the good choice because not many will go from reading magazine to searching in your Search Engine. Why should they, they have major Search Engines.

Billboards

Billboards are better but still just for people to remember your brand and of course they cover a territory. Pay per performance programs Pay per performance programs can only deliver you leads or affiliate signups. So no direct revenue.

Pay per click Search Engines

When you advertise in other Pay per Click Search Engines be sure how you do it and how high do you bid. Arrangements with web sites with a lot of traffic The best way to gain quality traffic is to partner with sites which have some content other then Search Engine or Directory.

Free Email Services, Personals, Shopping sites, organizations, etc.

Online Newsletters

Always stay in touch with your affiliates, partners and regular visitors. Send them with their permission quality newsletter time to time, announcements about contests you are planning, etc.

New equipment

Don't be to cheap to stay on old hardware keep up with new components and software.   Office You must be professional enough to have the office, don't do that from your garage or spare room. You can start small but as soon as you get enough money rent an office. Some Search Owners have offices if advertisers would see they'd never advertise with them. Software It's very important that you have customized software made by your own standards so everyone who will later work for you can fix that without any bigger problems. Otherwise you'd have a lot of problems and losses if you allow Software Engineers they can make programs their own way. Programmer does not hate anything more then fixing existing code.

Education

It is very important for you to keep up with all new things and you follow new inventions and trends in your branch. Why Pay per Click Search Engine Advertisers put all success on advertising in Search Engines, bigger is Search Engine and more is expensive happier they are, but after they see ROI their happiness fade away. It doesn't matter what kind of traffic Search
Engine delivers as long as is live and are not running scripts.

The best arrangement for Advertiser is click / unique IP / 24 hours only one Search Engine offers click / unique IP / 24 - 96 hours and non-incentive clicks. Everything else is irrelevant. Forget about foreign and domestic traffic. If there are real clicks this is not and issue, if they are incentive then you have a problem. Imagine you want to buy a boomerang and you'll search at some Australian Search Engine which doesn't allow foreign traffic, you wouldn't even see online stores with boomerang if you are not Australian.

Well those advertisers lost a customer because they advertise with wrong Search Engine. Test Search Engines with smaller amounts. Design your page with nice friendly design and make it user friendly, be clear and short with presentation, explain more later when customer notice you. If Search Engine send incentive visits arrange with Search Engine click / unique IP/ 24 – 96 hours and test it with small deposit. If ROI is still acceptable stay with it. Nobody can assure you is it good or not as long as you don't try it. Choose your keywords, it's not always true that the more keywords the better results.

You'll get more visitors that are true but ROI will be pore. If you advertise a dating service you'll for sure get more qualitative results with keyword personal, dating and match then with love lovers, date, flirt, married but looking, etc. Focus on content because Search Engines can only bring you visitors but you have to keep it.

Choose Search Engines or directories which have also other content at their site, so you'll begetting also visitors from other categories (Yahoo.com, MSN.com,Excite.com, Stonediver.com, Lycos.com, etc.) and/or Search Engines which are providing xml feed (bigger like Overture.com and smaller like Cockta.com and Cymicom.com) to other well visited Search Engines (bigger Altavista.com and Google.com, and smaller – whole list).

Choose your traffic The best system of course is to find a site (Stonediver.com) where you'll be able to choose your traffic and you'll be turning on and off your traffic providers as you please. You'll see the list of traffic sources and you'll check them out first and than turn them on or off. You'll be the one who decide what traffic, how much and when you'll be getting. More then testimonials, trust yourself, test it and convince yourself with results. It doesn't matter form where your traffic is coming as long as you make profit.

You must balance your budget, your wishes and which system will serve you better. Remember every source which brings you traffic with results – sales or membership is good source and it doesn't matter how lame the site may be. Online Traffic Broker Online Traffic Broker is the easiest way to start a business and anyone can do it. Advivid.com.

The easiest way where you can participate as Company who want to receive traffic or send traffic. You can negotiate with partners for down payment, advance payment, partial payment or credit. You can also set up conditions where partner have to pay you at least some percentage for traffic you sent.

If you want to get richer you'll have the chance, but first do something with the material you got. You can find details in book (Future Internet Gurus)

Now you are a millionaire! Well for how long? If you want riches the hard way, you might even keep the millions you earn very hard. If you were lucky down to your path, than be very careful with your money and investments.

1096518

Made in the USA